Into the Stillness

Dialogues on Awakening Beyond Thought

Gary Weber and Richard Doyle

NON-DUALITY PRESS
An Imprint of New Harbinger Publications

Gratitude to Suzanne Winters for her tireless efforts
on behalf of Stillness.

INTO THE STILLNESS
First edition published May 2015 by Non-Duality Press
©Gary Weber and Richard Doyle 2015

Non-Duality Press
An imprint of New Harbinger Publications

ISBN:
978-1-908664-53-2
www.newharbinger.com

FSC
www.fsc.org
MIX
Paper from
responsible sources
FSC® C011935

RAINFOREST ALLIANCE
CERTIFIED

Contents

A book has occurred

Rich: So, you know, strangeness. A book has occurred.

Gary: Strangeness. A book has manifested out of thin air.

R: It's totally unbelievable. Where did it come from?

G: Well the whole thing came out of no place, as you know. It just arose in meditation that we should do some dialogues. So we started doing dialogues and they clicked.

R: And then somehow they manifest out of the Stillness and it's like a book just popped up out of the void, or out of the nothing, out of the Stillness. What should people do with it?

G: Well, we've talked many times… the good thing about it is that it's spontaneous. But we've found out that as we do this thing what emerges from each one of us moves into something that's much larger; $1 + 1 = 3\,\frac{1}{2}$ or something. So stuff that we didn't know we knew is in this video and in the dialogues.

R: So that can happen to other people: they can pick up the book and engage in the dialogue and experience the dialogue. And they don't really need to begin or start anywhere in particular.

G: Any place, any page will work, any dialogue will work. They're equally useful… or not.

R: I even think you can start mid-dialogue, you know, just open it. It's like the book is designed for bibliomancy…

G: Oh yes, exactly. Any place in the book will work.

R: Just dip into it, start riffling…

G: Well, we've talked about this idea of showing people how to do dialogue, which is something that people don't do much anymore… given that we're doing this (*texting with thumbs*) all day long, we don't spend much time trying to get into dialogue with somebody. We're just so afraid to have an open discussion without anybody feeling threatened and just let the whole thing unwind its way out.

R: Indeed, you know when I'm teaching and I talk about dialogue in the classroom, I've found that people think dialogue is what you do to avoid fighting. (*Laughter*)

R: Like where we get together and figure out how we can agree, and that's not what it is! It's an exploration.

G: Ahhhh, that's great!

R: Isn't that funny?

G: It is! But it is having that confidence, a fundamental trust in each other, and enough self-confidence and awareness to be able to just work your way through this stuff, piece by piece, and kind of feel your way into what the next thing is as it comes up.

R: And it's practice in strengthening the "letting go" muscle because you can just let go into it, don't try to anticipate what the other person is saying—just hear it and respond.

G: And see what comes up.

R: And when we do that it's like a practice for filling our self with Presence all the time. Just feel what the refrigerator door feels like when we open it. See what the light looks like inside. Taste what the onion tastes like when we're cooking it. It's the same thing isn't it?

G: Yes, it's a very tactile thing. It's the feel of what it feels like to be in dialogue, to be the emptiness and just feeling something come up out of no place as the next thing to be manifested.

R: Sometimes I feel like what we're going through is actually a re-awakening of feeling. Not feeling in the sense of an "emotion"—but that somehow we've been through this period where we've atrophied the sense of access to the flow of what comes from that no place. It's still there, but you have to sort of look for it and use it and practice it. It's an inner feeling? It's the sensing of what it feels like inside.

G: Oh, totally. We've talked about how it's very important in this work, since a lot of it is DIY, to get a good sense for when things feel like they aren't working anymore; what they felt like before, and what they feel like now. Have things gotten flat? You can feel that in a tactile way, as you can do with this work. You can feel if you're in honest, authentic dialogue or you can feel yourself being inauthentic. Can you feel yourself not coming out fully with what you want to say, or what is manifesting for you? Or do you hold back?

R: So by following along with our letting go, other people can learn to let go.

G: Let go of themselves… just trust the process and surrender to your Self.

R: So, who wrote this book?

G: It came from no place. One of the mysteries is just how do these things write themselves? This book came out of no place. The initiative to do it just arose in meditation and we just said well, let's do a dialogue and see what happens. You had set it up within a space of three or four days and we had found somebody to do it with and we had found a filming studio… it just manifested.

R: Miraculous even.

G: Miraculous!

R: But of course everything is miraculous because everything comes out of this place, which is no place.

G: It does!

R: But in this case it was obvious, it was very obvious. If there are any royalties who should we send them to?

G: I don't know where it goes to, because really, as we've observed, there is nobody doing this speaking. It's just coming out of no place, spontaneously, and we get synergies out of it; $1 + 1 = 3$.

R: It's only insofar as each of us gets out of the way that it emerges so...

G: Yes.

R: It's not us speaking.

G: No.

R: But something else speaking forth...

G: Right. Things we don't know we knew, come up and they join together in a way that's much more powerful than either individual speech.

R: Indeed. I'm convinced we didn't know. You know what I mean?

G: We didn't even know it.

R: It isn't just that we knew it and didn't know it. It's that by creating this space knowledge emerges.

G: It may also be that we had pieces and parts in different parts of the brain, and as we start to do this we call upon whatever the topic is, it goes out and grabs pieces and puts together a story. Out of that comes something that we hadn't known before, or at least it hadn't been organized in quite that way, and it matches with what you're saying and then you do the same thing. So the pieces were there, they just weren't assembled in a coherent way.

R: That's why it's going to be interesting to see what pieces people pull out of the book. It's going to be a situation where they get pulled like a magnet to this dialogue or that line or this line. It will differ individually. Then to see what they make of it. It's going to be like a mashup of our mashup.

G: Well, one of your favorite words is "bibliomancy", and in fact this will be an ideal text for that. We can just pick it up, open it at any page, any line, any paragraph, and it may be useful to you. It came out of us spontaneously.

R: It's almost as if it's a book written for bibliomancy. Most books are not written for bibliomancy. It's against the grain.

G: Right.

R: But this one, you just pick it up, you open it, you look, you see what it's saying… you feel the response in you. Then you feel the response in whoever is responding in the text. Now you've got three responses happening. You can start to tune your own ability to let go into that response.

G: It came out of the space. Speaking about feeling, we've talked a lot about feeling, about getting a sense of what it feels like to come from down in here (*chest*) as opposed to coming out of here (*head*). If you come from down in here (*chest*) out of Stillness, something of a whole different quality emerges. That's what this is. This is full of those individual pieces coming out of who-knows-where place and putting them together. If you can read that and get that same sense of it, you can feel in yourself something coming out of your own space.

R: You can feel that—it's a very particular feeling, or the very particular absence of other feelings. It's going to be interesting to see what people do with it.

G: It could be a very useful book.

R: So what is the context for this book?

G: An important aspect is, as we talked about in the episodes as well, that there is no context. We aren't trying to set a context. We don't have a set and setting that we're coming from or moving into. We just let whatever manifests come out. Something else, or some "energy else", is creating its own context. This is just manifesting out of that. There is no storyline, there's no message, there's just coming out and it doing itself.

R: How should other people understand it then?

G: Just recognize that this is completely spontaneous. There is no precognition, there's no premeditation. It just comes out of no place. People are amazed that it can happen but it does happen. We're still speaking in voices or tongues; it's just coming out of nowhere, coherent as it is, with no background, no setting, and no storyline.

R: That is the context then.

G: That is the context.

R: In other words, if you want to understand this book, use the book to get to that place where things are coming out of Stillness. So the Stillness is the context.

G: Yes. If it has a purpose, the purpose would be to get people in the situation to recognize that they can work this way themselves. They can feel the energy in the book of spontaneous speaking and feel it in themselves; they can manifest exactly that same thing. We (Gary and Rich) are not particularly empowered this way. Anybody can do this. They just get out of the way and feel it coming from down here (*points to belly/chest*) not up here (*points to head*) and just wait for it, be present, be patient and let it come out. It's astonishing what can happen.

R: In fact it's the only way they've ever created anything anyway.

Predestination, control, free will and the illusion of time

R: So, has all of cosmic history been leading up to this dialogue on predestination?

G: Yes. Everything since the big bang has conspired to bring us to this very point at this time.

R: I'm not quite sure how you come up with that logic but maybe we can examine it a little bit.

G: Yes. If you just look back at our lives, and think how many things had to take place before now—in your life, and in mine, to come to this point at this time. Not that this is the *only* best place in the whole world...

R: But it's where I am.

G: But it's where you are, it's where you are. And arguably, if almost any one thing of thousands of things—perhaps millions of things—in your past had been different, you wouldn't be here right now. You're not aware of those; you can't—nobody can—go back and cognize all of the possibilities and choices that were made some time in the past that led you to be right here at this point at this time.

If your grandma had gotten on a different bus or had gone to a different party or your grandfather had gone some other path that day, you wouldn't be here today. We certainly wouldn't be here together today. So you get into the consideration of what do you take out of the entire stream of events that brought you here to this point that wouldn't matter?

And the difficulty is, that you don't know which one of those really did matter, and how much it changed everything that came after.

R: Right. This is what the time travel theme in science fiction stories always get into... which event can change in the past without the present disappearing? As we've discussed, that makes a lot of sense in terms of deconstructing the idea that we are in control.

Because you know that when you look at the past or you look at your involvement in an event that unfolds in the near future, you can see that there's just way too much complexity there for you to possibly have made that a decision to cause yourself to come into being. The long and the short of it is, did you decide when you were going to be born?

G: Right.

R: No. Are you going to decide when you're going to die?

G: No.

R: No. So that seems to me that if we'll really look at it, we'll see that this illusion of control that the "I" has is just that, it's an illusion. It's a kind of a cursor that we use to move through the world and maybe in certain evolutionary situations it was favored. But it's not the case that we exert control. It may be sexy to other primates to make it seem like we were in control, but we're not in control.

G: Right.

R: But there's a more subtle philosophical question. Just because we're not in control doesn't mean that everything is predestined, right? In other words, we can imagine a lot of scenarios on the continuum between total chaos and total order where, true enough there's too much complexity for our "I" (if it existed) to be in control.

But how does that play into this idea that everything is predetermined when we can't even predict, for example, when a drop of water is going to drop out of a faucet because of the sensitivity of that drop of water to initial conditions? So it seems to me there's another piece of that discussion that has to happen. You were alluding to it before, but another piece of that discussion has to happen in order to feel the truth of the predestination aspect.

G: It's funny how different people feel about the three things. If you ask, "Well, are you in control of every facet of your life?" almost nobody will say "yes". They've all been through natural disasters, seen calamities, family members have died, they've seen car wrecks that clearly were out of their control. So then they say, "Okay, I'm not in control of everything in my life, but for some things I am."

R: I can choose fries rather than onion rings.

G: I can choose fries, not onion rings. Or I can choose the small drink or the big drink.

R: Right, super-size it.

G: Yes. But those come to the same thing though. Which one of those choices that I can make were unimportant? They say, "Well if I can't control that, what can I control?" And the problem with choice and control is that we don't know the implications of our decision. I make a decision which takes five seconds more in line at the Thai restaurant or wherever. Just 5 or 10 seconds longer in line. At some level that has perturbed the entire universe. Everybody's universe has been moved by five seconds because of my five second delay. All of their universes are moving at the same time.

We don't know who that might impact. Some other diner might have been there, who then went out in the street five seconds later and got hit by a car. Their whole family's lives changed. We just don't know what the implications are of any action that we did. As far as my saying that I know what's going to happen from my actions, I don't. Because 3, 4, 5 days down the road many, many thousands of things could have happened that were perturbed by my seemingly insignificant decision.

R: But you see how that could actually be an argument against predestination then. Because the present does not allow us to know what the future is going to be, precisely because it's not determined.

G: But you can't step out of it. I mean, the thing is that nobody can step out of the dance. We presume that if it isn't predestined, we can step out of the dance. And if I step out of the dance then everybody has to wait on me to do something before the dance can go on.

R: No, that's not what I intended. I mean, so, we give up personal control, individual personal control.

G: Okay.

R: And so we are dancing along and buffeted even, by all the events that are happening absolutely everywhere in the cosmos since the beginning. Whether or not those events themselves are deterministic is then, it seems to me, a different question. For me, the reason why they appear to be deterministic is, because what you're alluding to is that, if everything is one thing, then that includes past, present, future… that there is no openness in the future. It's all already happened as it were…

G: But it doesn't have to have already happened. The argument to me is that there are your two poles—it's either completely chaotic, or completely ordered. And I don't have any sense in my life that my life is chaotic. On the contrary, my life is massively serendipitous… I can watch things being arranged

—or arranging themselves—in an astonishing way: such low probability events occur in my life, and over and over and day by day by day. And so, I don't think it's just me... most of us, if we can just step back and watch, can see that our life is highly serendipitous.

R: Sure.

G: Arranged by?

R: They wouldn't be here if it wasn't.

G: They wouldn't be here if it wasn't. If it was just chaos then you know we'd be just as likely to be sitting over in that corner never seeing each other again. And that isn't the case, that isn't what happens. So there is a lot of predestination in our lives to bring us from minute to minute to second, second, second. So if I gotta choose between chaos and predestination, predestination or order—let's just say order first.

R: Yeah.

G: Order is certainly obvious to me... and those seem to be logically the only two choices. And so if I've got order then I say well, do I have any ability to change the order myself? Can I change order? Well, not discretely, to your point. I can't step out, alone, of this massive interconnected universe and say "I'm going to make a decision different from what's moving through the dance." There can't be a possibility to do that because we've got 7 billion people right now running around the planet. If everybody was able to step out of the dance, we're back into chaos again. So to keep this web working, logically it follows, to me at least, that there has to be some way that we cannot step out of the dance. If we could the whole thing could disintegrate.

R: No, we definitely can't step out of the dance precisely because of our interconnection with each other and with the cosmos. But I think this question about predestination comes into focus when we say, "Are the only two choices total disorder and total order?" Or is it that what's unfolding is different levels of order, that we have a kind of emergent experience of order where not even the system knows what is going to happen? Not even the cosmos itself knows what is going to happen. Which undermines the idea of it being predestined in the usual sense that we mean that, right?

G: Well, maybe it's a question of temporal scale.

R: Yeah.

G: Everything's predestined from the beginning of the Big Bang to the end of this next collapse, which is, you know, n billion years in the future. You don't need that. For me it's as if we have an anthropomorphic all Oneness/She. If there is the Universal field we can see everything as one thing. And if the Higgs field or whatever name we're going to use for the Universal field exists—and we think we have the Higgs field pretty well defined now—if that is self-aware, but we have no indication that the Higgs field is self-conscious. We have no way of knowing that. But you could posit that if there is an All-Thingness that is self-aware, as many scientists are saying, then everything gets explained. Quantum mechanics gets explained, collapse at the electron level gets explained, and this very question gets explained. Because She doesn't have to know that far out. All She has to know is this far out. And She is local as well as non-local; She is learning and seeing each moment by moment. We are not in charge of that thing. That doesn't mean there isn't something...

R: That's it.

G: ... that is all-knowing that is beyond my very humble intelligence and capabilities that is in fact dancing this thing picosecond by picosecond. That's the part that we can't step out of. That's the part that's predetermined. Not a billion years in the future...

R: Right.

G: ... but the next picosecond is not within anybody's control except the Universal field.

R: Well that's where this experience of Oneness is really the major premise of this argument. If you experience Oneness and you experience synchronicity, then it becomes obvious that, at least at the scale that we exist on, everything is unfolding exactly as it should...

G: Perfectly.

R: ... as it were. But if you don't experience that Oneness then you think that the future is somehow separate from the present...

G: Right.

R: ... Right, that there's a dualism between the present and the future. And because we can't know what is going to exist with that drop of water as it drops in the next however many picoseconds, then it's unknown. But what's interesting is to experiment with in terms of whether or not the Higgs field is self-aware, is that we can sort of shift that question a little bit. We can know that in a way it's self-aware because we know about it, and we are an attribute of that field, rather than in any possible way separate from it.

G: Right.

R: So, if we know about the Higgs field[1] and all of cosmic history can be experimented with as the unfolding of our

1.The Higgs field is an energy field that exists everywhere in the universe. It is accompanied by a fundamental particle called the Higgs boson, which the field "uses" to interact with other particles continuously.

knowledge of what we really are, which is an attribute of this Higgs field...

G: Right.

R: ... then it's not a stretch at all to say, "Well of course it has self-awareness, that's how we know what it is!" As opposed to the dualist perspective which would say, "Well, how do we know that that is self-aware?" Right? Well if we could separate the Higgs field from us, well then of course we can't really get our mind around the idea that it is or isn't self-aware.

G: We can't.

R: But if we can't be separated from it, and it appears to be the case that we are aware...

G: Right.

R: ... then of course it has self-awareness.

G: ... and it is incontestably all-pervasive. Nobody's saying it isn't all-pervasive.

R: All-pervasive, manifests matter...?

G: Yes, we know that part.

R: What else do we know about it?

G: We know it's all-pervasive, we know it actually makes matter come into being.

R: And, we know that we're conscious.

G: We know we're conscious.

R: So you put those three things together and what seems like a kind of wildly unwarranted speculation that there's an attribute of the cosmos itself that pervades all things and is itself conscious...

G: Right.

R:...becomes instead something that can be observed empirically...

G: Right...

R: Oneself!

G: Almost "Duh?"

R: Yes.

G: But then also you mentioned in addition to the importance of, the value of, being able to see that everything is one thing, you can also see that our perception of time is an illusion.

R: Yes.

G: Where you fall out of the sense of time, and live only in now. Not just because Eckhart Tolle says that. There only is now. There's never a past or a future that you can really grasp, it's old stored stuff which is...

R: It's now again.

G: It's now again, it's now again. That changes the point about the speculation about long-term predestination. I think our predestination is zero—except other than the fact that the field is moving, modifying, picosecond by picosecond. And when you get out of this having a sense of time, then that's much more apparent to you. In fact you can grok that... "Yeah, I get this!" The field is continuously reformatting, changing, and modifying itself picosecond by picosecond.

R: So this looking at predestination helps us come up against the fact that the future itself is a kind of fiction because it relies on the separation of ourselves from present moment.

G: Right, right.

R: And if we dwell in present moment the question of pre-destination doesn't even arise.

G: No.

R: Because we just *are*.

G: Right. And there's no sense of time. Without a sense of time the whole idea of predestination doesn't mean anything.

R: Exactly.

G: There's just now, now, now, now, now, unfolding.

R: And the feeling of predestination is, "I have always been, and I always will be."

G: Right… right. Yes.

R: Useful.

Using dialogue for awakening...

R: So Gary, we've been doing these dialogues, and of course we haven't required any instruction manual or it hasn't required us to come to some sort of pre-given destination or definition for the dialogues. But I thought it might be useful to talk about what dialogue *is* and why it's such a useful tool. I found it to be a very useful tool in my own path; it's not one I see recommended very often.

G: It's an interesting pedagogical approach as these discussions aren't rehearsed; we don't come up with anything ahead of time or have any script to follow. You and I both found that there's a lot of learning that takes place just by virtue of opening up to let what manifests, manifest. Out of that sharing comes something better than either one of us could have thought up. This is a learning process. It's really a great practice to be open enough that you don't encumber what's coming out of you, and you just let it respond to the gestalt of the energy that's unfolding at that time. There's no scripting, no organizer, no *I shouldn't say this* or *I shouldn't say that...* it just comes out.

R: Right. Somebody can say, "Oh well, you know that's exactly what people do in psychoanalysis," but there's something qualitatively different about real dialogue. If you're going into psychoanalysis, which is not something I'm criticizing, there's a hierarchical difference between the patient and the analyst.

G: Oh, absolutely! And there's also a template.

R: Yeah.

G: The psychoanalyst comes in with a box to put you in. "I've been trained as a Freudian, a Jungian or a transpersonal psychologist, and this is my box I have for you." So he listens to what you're saying—using this template. And he says, well, this fits in here, this fits in there and this fits in there, and so his response to you is out of that template. He doesn't give space for you to be empty, and for also for him to not have a template.

If you don't have a template as a psychoanalyst, then something else comes out that's very different. They are training people on the West Coast in San Francisco to be "non-dual" psychotherapists. The idea being to just get out of the way. Just don't be there, just be empty, and like we're doing, just see what comes up. It's astonishing what can result.

R: What's so beautiful is that then, when you're engaged in the dialogue, it's really a practice of emptiness...

G: Yes!

R: ... because you're just being empty instead of saying, well he's going to say this, so then I should say that. It's a really helpful incentive towards being empty instead of a continued goad towards coming up with something to say. It's the exact opposite of that.

One of the benefits is that it's a kind of search engine for finding those things that you are having trouble emptying. It goes right to the place where you may be holding onto something or you have queries about something. Instead of rehearsing what it is that you should talk about, or adopting a teaching and then incorporating that teaching into your practice (which all have virtues), I found that this clarity and work of dialogue in a more or less peer-to-peer way with mutual respect and mutual emptiness worked well for me. I don't know how anything else could have gotten me through a lot of the things that I went through.

G: Yes. Well you have to trust that what comes out of emptiness will be "okay". As you start to trust and you say, "Well, I'll just let this come out". Then it comes out and you say, "That's really good, that's pretty cool." Then you begin to trust that process to a point where you begin to trust it completely, and you get to where you don't ever interpolate your discussion. It just comes out as it comes out, and it's much more fluid, insightful and useful than what we'd have done if we had scripted it, tried to manage it to make sure the right thing is said or not the wrong thing.

You've talked about levels. It's very important if you're going to have a dialogue (*hands level with each other*), to not have a hierarchy (*one hand high and one hand low*). You have to be at the same level. That you're actually equally open to whatever the other person has to say and you're just letting it dance however it dances. I also found that exchanging money makes a big difference. If you pay me two hundred fifty or three hundred dollars an hour to talk to me, then that really does change our relationship.

R: Yes, let's get past this. There's something I need to talk to you about and (*taps watch impatiently*)... (*laughs*)

G: (*laughs*) Time is up, time is up!

R: Oh, we didn't get to it!

G: Yes. As soon as you put money on the table, with some hierarchy to justify it ... "I am a learned person, here're my degrees from Columbia, and you're coming in to see me." Then that's a whole different thing. How you can get an open, free-flowing exchange of information in that situation? You can't!

R: No, but that's what's interesting is that dialogue itself often seems to be almost impossible because we don't have an infrastructure. We don't have any framework for people just to meet up as equals, practice emptiness and exchange where they are, which is in Oneness. But we can imagine some scenarios where that could be at least cultivated, right? We've talked a little bit about this idea of peer-to-peer dialogue using web tools to help organize getting people together to do this. You're quite right that if it just becomes the specialty of a couple of people, then supply and demand...

Let's say somebody becomes really great at dialogue. Let's say Gary Weber becomes famous for his *Dialogue Method*. Hey exactly, you're rolling your eyes! But then all of a sudden, the successful teacher then gets too many people! Then they use money to manage it. Well, I can't see everybody, every day, so I'll make it three hundred dollars, make it three hundred fifty dollars.

G: Oh and they do!

R: Exactly!

G: And they do.

R: So there has to be some way to deal with supply and demand. But the premise is that we're all in that position where we can be ready to give emptiness and dialogue to another person if we're willing.

G: Right.

R: As long as it becomes something that is a specialty of somebody, then we're going to have a supply and demand problem. But if people begin practicing it on their own, without needing to be certified through any academy or justified by anything, but just practicing it, then pretty soon you're going to be able to see that we all have somebody that if we want to, we can go to and do this. It might be worth thinking about what some protocols for that would be.

G: To me the fascinating thing is that you can feel in yourself if you're being authentic. You can feel as soon as you move into a script, into, "Oh, he said something and I'm this and I'm..." You can just feel how subtle and how quick that shift is, and how the energy inside changes. It isn't like you need any kind of a monitor to watch and see if you're being authentic or not. You know yourself.

R: You *are* that monitor.

G: You are the monitor! You know as soon as you're being inauthentic and you can feel that. The other person can feel it too. As soon as you change the structure and charge money, somebody gets all puffed up...

People will get all excited about themselves, and if they get money, then, "Oooh, I can get more money! Well this guy's getting more money than I am, so I want even more money than he gets!" The whole thing gets crazy. Then you're no longer authentic, you stop being in dialogue. Then you are totally different. It's not dialogue, it's a monologue.

R: So the commitment has to be this commitment to total emptiness.

G: Authenticity.

R: Yes.

G: Complete authenticity with no barriers, no interruptions, nobody mediating or interpreting anything that comes out. Whatever comes out of the great Emptiness is what's being said.

R: Most of the time, even in the philosophical tradition, we think of dialogue as people exchanging knowledge. In fact, what you're pointing to is the fact that what we're doing is creating the conditions of *not knowing*; dialogue is a tool for not knowing.

G: Absolutely! Yes. A critical thing... we *have* to not know.

We both have to not know what we're going to say, not know our stance on the subject, and just let whatever comes out, come out of that not knowing space, absolutely.

R: When you're committed to not knowing, then even when you know and you fall into a script of some kind, which is going to happen, then the other person is there to call out the script, and say, "It feels like a script." There are many ways to respond. If this was a software that was free and widely available by which...

G: Open source...

R: Open source dialogue, exactly! By which people could pursue awakening beyond thought, then it would be getting downloaded...

G: That's right, that'd be good.

R: I have a feeling that because it's right in front of us, we don't see that it's the most powerful tool that we have at our disposal.

G: I believe, too, that people are afraid to trust that they can just say what comes out and let it go out there. They are worried, "Oh my goodness, what are they gonna think of me if I say this thing or that thing?" You've got to get to the place where you can trust that, be open to it, and if you feel that inauthenticity, that scripting, coming in, you can just let go of it. You can just surrender that. As you do, then openness manifests.

Can you "do nothing" and awaken?

R: Nothing, I've got nothing to say. But I've got a whole lot of nothing! Okay! (*laughs*)

G: (*laughs*) How about, there's nothing you need to do to awaken? This is one of the big—in my humble opinion—misconceptions that gives non-duality a bad name, especially with people who have done a lot of meditation like my Buddhist friends. This seems disingenuous. Thought maybe we could talk about that some.

R: Sure. I mean we can talk about its truth value first so we can get that out of the way. It's absolutely true that nothing has to be done for you to awaken. But probably there's a way better chance of you awakening if something is done. Like, it is possible, it's true, you could just wait to be getting on a bus and have your entire self-referential thought turn off as it happened to Suzanne Segal?

G: But she had practiced... a lot.

R: She had practiced an enormous amount! Yes, but that's not significant. I mean really, all you really need to do is wait...

G: All you need to do is get on and off a bus.

R: ... in fact what you ought to do is maybe get on and off the bus a lot.

G: A lot.

R: That way you're going to increase the likelihood that it's going to happen.

G: Problem of it is you could spend a long time doing it.

R: Or you could say, stroll across a park...

G: That's right.

R: And...

G: Just do it enough times.

R: Yes, enough times.

G: You'll wake up.

R: Then you'll wake up. Or, you could listen to the diverse and various traditions that have been practicing this for eons and find which aspects of those traditions seem to work for you, and see if practicing doesn't actually yield some immediate feedback.

G: Yes, we know now, especially in the last 6 or 8 years, because there's a great deal of research on training effects for every skill you can think of—from violin to chess to surgery to firefighting. The more you practice the better you get at it. The brain needs repetition to be able to get efficient at doing a particular task.

We know that from riding a bicycle. Your first time on a bicycle is a traumatic event; you're wobbling around, the brain's highly engaged (if you could scan that). Later, when you become very proficient, you can text, balance, no-hands and carry groceries, but that's with a lot of training. This magical 10,000 hour thing that Malcolm Gladwell came up with in one of his books, *Outliers: The Story of Success*, which really represents K. Anders Ericsson's work from Florida State, which is very thorough and complete, says exactly that. That—forget the genius thing—every high performer, every expert, every adept, had much, much, much practice before that. As you pointed out though, it's not like nothing happens. It's not like you're practicing the violin and nothing happens until 10,000 hours and you suddenly…

R: All of a sudden!

G: … all of a sudden you're playing fantastically well!

R: Give me my Stradivarius now! (*laughs*)

G: (*laughs*) Exactly, because in the whole process of—if you ever do 10,000 hours—in the process of moving up that ladder, you get better and better and the music gets better and you can play more sophisticated things and more complicated things. But to say, "Here's this guy, he's playing fantastically well. He never had to practice!" is naïve. It just isn't the truth.

R: Yes, it's bizarre. That's why I said it is true, under one understanding of the sentence "you have to do nothing in order to become awakened" that, yes, you have to do lots, and lots, and lots of nothing. My son, for example, plays the violin, and he's quite good for a 12 year old. In order to play the violin, he has to enter something like a non-dual state. If he thinks about where his fingers are going to go as he's learning a piece, he messes up and becomes frustrated. That frustration is the self-referential self, saying, "Hey, why can't you do this?" instead of just being *with* the violin, allowing his fingers to move, building on past practice and continuing that practice in the future. In order for him to perfect a piece, he has to get out of the way of the piece—of his body completing the piece, which means he needs to learn how to—from the perspective of a self-referential thought—do nothing, rigorously. This doesn't mean that the violin isn't getting played, that his body is not being trained in the various movements; on the contrary.

So, if we want to take this "do nothing" approach to awakening seriously, we can say, "Yes, but you have to do so very rigorously" which means incorporating that non-dual state, or the approach to it, into any practice, whatsoever. Probably if you looked at those 10,000 hour examples, at some point in that process people will come into the awareness either implicitly or explicitly that they need to get out of the way for it to happen.

G: But it doesn't happen all by itself.

R: No.

G: It's like when I think back to my many, many, many hours of sitting meditation and doing yoga, to your point, I routinely sat long enough, like 35 minutes, until something really good happens. In my experience in meditation at about 35 minutes, there is something like a runner's high which kicks in. I'm sure it's neurotransmitters... some kind of pleasurable release. As far as we can ascertain, this "runner's high" and the "shift" which is more permanent, are both generated primarily by endogenous dopamine. The more permanent shift eventually has an increasingly different and sweeter feel, which the experts in the field believe is from increasing levels of endogenous opiates. But back to your point, I had to practice for 34 minutes to get to this place to where I dropped into this non-dual state of Oneness, of there being no "other". It, of course, then lasted for increasingly longer times but then it shut back down again.

But it seems like, although we haven't proven this yet, that the more of those pictures the brain can get and the better the pictures are... if it is a picture of, "Wow, that was really cool!", then the brain seems to say, "We'll start working on that." I always sat, day after day after day, until I got to that space. I just never stopped until I got to that space. The brain just kept seeing that and said, "Hey this is cool!" and, "We'll re-functionalize for that." But you're correct, it's a lot of practice each time and then you'll hope to get to a short period of transcendence. But you need to get to where it's also a reward for your practice. You do get something good back out of your practice. It's like training a pet.

R: In other words, "nothing" is the accomplishment. There's an ambiguity in what is being referred to. "You don't need to do anything in order to achieve awareness" is a misunderstanding of the perspective that that's actually the achievement. The achievement is you not doing anything.

From my son's perspective, he certainly feels like he has to go and practice his violin and it's not always the top thing on his agenda. This idea that there's nothing that you need to do, maybe to be charitable about it, is a kind of retroactive illusion. That after you've achieved a certain kind of state, the call is less insistent to go and sit until you feel that mode of awareness because the mode of awareness is already here! Then you say, "Well gosh! That mode of awareness has always been here, I know that it is the very substrate of my consciousness. If only I'd known back in the day, I would have just looked at it and experienced it!" Yes, but…

G: But you couldn't have though.

R: Exactly.

G: Yes, and I think that's what the misinterpretation is now. People who are out there and living in that space say, "There's nothing you have to do to awaken. Look, I'm sitting here, I have to do nothing to awaken and I'm sitting in that space." But then people read that and say "Well, I'll just sit here and do nothing." And they really do nothing, not the kind of "do nothing" you're talking about, they really do nothing and then nothing happens. Then they convince themselves philosophically that they've somehow reached some kind of a state. Maybe they've had an experience some time in the past and they believe now that, "Oh, I really understand," but they don't. They haven't done the work to get to those repetitive "do nothings" until they finally live there.

R: Or an equally problematic outcome is that they come to the conclusion that there is actually nothing to all this, that there is no such state that people are experiencing, and that it's just a scam.

G: Right. That's an emerging external view which I mentioned up front, of the non-dual community that it is increasingly voicing that there's nothing you have to do. But the people who have meditated a long time, say, "Well that's not true because I did all these things, this happened and I had to learn into this thing and now it's fantastic." To believe you just have to do nothing at all, no practice, is just incorrect... disingenuous.

R: Yes. It's hard work to "do nothing" actually. You have to do hard work to get to nothing.

G: To get to "nothing", yes. The same thing happens with running. You're a runner... and all runners have seen the same thing... You run for a while and the "runner's high" kicks in, and you're into this fantastically neurotransmitter-reinforced blissful state and there's nothing there, except there's just pleasure taking place. Many runners run to that place.

R: If you're a runner or a swimmer where you get to that place, you don't then say, "Well gosh, I didn't need to do those first fifty laps in order to get to this. I should have just been in this right away!"

G: (laughs) Exactly! I'd have jumped in the water and been here. It doesn't work.

R: It's not possible. You just jump in the water and wait for the feeling to arrive... it's not going to happen.

G: That's right. It doesn't happen.

Why do we fear emptiness, silence and stillness?

G: How about we discuss *Sunyata*, the traditional translation of parts of the *Heart Sutra*[2], what our experience is of non-dual awakening and what is often translated as "the Void" from the Buddhist texts?

R: What's interesting is that on the one hand it can be helpful because if I translate *Sunyata* as zero, I can think that I'm practicing in order to achieve a kind of zero state of my self-referential thought. That doesn't mean that what is experienced then is a zero state, to the contrary. The way I used to put it to myself, rather early on in my practice when I was really starting to get results, was you have to go to zero to find the One. You have to make zero in order to see how to experience unity. I think the translation of 'Void' or 'emptiness' is really unfortunate because it makes people feel like what they're looking for is nothingness, when the experience is fullness itself because you're getting out of the way of the cosmos itself.

G: The whole thing about 'form is emptiness, emptiness is form', is to disabuse people of the belief that this is an empty dark void of the worst possible existential kind you can imagine. I think that scares people away from all of the practices because they think they're going to get to zero—to a bleak nothingness. I don't know why the Buddha did it the way he did it. He seemingly took that discussion off the table, just as a teaching tool, to get a perspective, just to look at what

2. www.en.wikipedia.org/wiki/Heart_Sutra

23

we can validate.

R: Yes, don't speculate about what's there, just look.

G: Just look, just look directly. So he didn't postulate a different explanation for that state that would be sweeter. But in my experience it's a very sweet space. It may be that when you first land in it, it's still a little bit uncertain, not quite so sweet but it's not bad. I did not see any Dark Night of the Soul. There's a lot of Dark Night of the Soul stuff around right now. I didn't see one. Many people haven't seen one; it's not required.

It tends to be, in my experience, heavily correlated with a Christian upbringing and how deeply you were imbued with the belief that there was a Dark Night of the Soul.

But the state of Stillness and Oneness first comes in as kind of a medium place, and, in my experience, it gets sweeter and sweeter and sweeter with time. It looks like it's primarily our own dopamine at first and then the sweetness is added by our own opioids.

R: Right. In the Tibetan tradition they have the translation *rigpa* for 'clear awareness.' "Buddha nature" is another way of thinking about it. The problem with this language of emptiness and void is, as you pointed out, that it makes it less likely that people are actually going to look and get still enough to be with it—to be at ease with it.

It feels like they're going to have to "face the abyss". Well yes, from an egoic perspective it's what the ego thinks is an abyss, because the ego wants to take credit for everything that's coming into existence, so it says, "All that's comin' out of nothin'! There's nothin' there. If it weren't for me, then you're just gonna see that abyss!"

But if you can tarry with that "abyss" you can see that it's anything but that. One of the people that I found useful for my own framework was Franklin Merrell-Wolff, the early twentieth century mathematician and philosopher. He was interested in the nature of consciousness and found that mathematics serves as a bridge between the relative and the transcendental. He describes the abyss very clearly in what he called one of his "realizations."

He abstracted the subjective moment from the so-called "objective manifold" of consciousness. He looked at the little bit that he *was* and said that, of course, at first it appeared as darkness because our senses are used to looking out into the world, looking out at that "objective manifold", so when we look within we don't see it, and in not seeing that, at first it seems like it's darkness. But then he says, "I very quickly saw that it was light and fullness." It's only the initial glance that may be challenging, because it's different from the outside nature of reality—it's *not* that.

If we can have even the tiniest bit of patience to look at that so-called abyss we see that it is the Source of all things. The more you're able to experience that it is the Source of all things, your ego can take less and less credit for what's going on in the world. To me, the experiences I've had of nervousness, anxiety, paranoia or darkness, as you were putting it, were really a response from my egoic self that didn't like where this was going. (*laughs*)

G: Oh yes, this is not on the ego's Christmas list.

R: No!

G: The last thing the ego wants to have happen is to be out of a job.

R: But even the ego is misinformed about the nature of this space, because as you know, I've given my ego quite an important job. It's the *Executive Vice President of Neurodynamic Inventory and Control,* and anytime self-referential thoughts occur, it has the very important job of taking those referential thoughts, seeking their source and returning them there.

G: Exactly.

R: It's a very important job! Without that job I couldn't stay in the Source.

G: There's even the great fear around not having thoughts. I was a classic Type A personality, guilty of that. I believed, because I was a knowledge worker, that if my thoughts stopped I would literally, literally die. I was absolutely convinced that I would just die. We're trained to believe that thoughts are really necessary. But, you find out that it isn't even close to being true.

In the course of a night we have some dreamless sleep and we don't have thoughts. When we wake up in the morning, there's a space where we don't have thoughts. In between thoughts, we don't have thoughts. Thoughts are not (*beeeeeeeeeep*)—there's a break between thoughts. We're so conditioned to believe that we have to have these things. People say, "Oh if I lose my thoughts (like I did) you will die! Something awful will happen. You'll lie in the gutter. There's no hope for you." In fact that's absolutely not true!

R: That's especially the case for people who are making their living with ideas, which, unlike thoughts, do not stop. They become more available—paradoxically. Again it's this idea, "Well, that's all well and good but I make my living off of thoughts," or "I am my thoughts" is what's really…

G: And that's really true. No, ultimately it is true. The "I" is…

R: The "I" itself is thought.

G: … is thought.

R: But that's not the whole person who's experiencing them. To me it's akin to the language of "ego-death" that was often used in the psychological literature of the sixties and seventies to describe psychedelic experience and other manifestations of the reality of Source. It's rhetorically unfortunate because it sends the message that there's something very negative going on, when the opposite is true. It's the sweetest, fullest, most loving, caring, and manifesting experience that anyone could ever wish for. It's what we are looking for in drugs or in sex or material accomplishment or even love of another human being. It is actually what is right in us, which, if we will learn how to focus our awareness on it, will begin to manifest more and more.

G: We confuse the processes by which we get into this space as *causing* this space. In fact all they do is allow you to get out of the way, whether it's any of the things you mentioned or anything else. To get you to that space, we do all kinds of crazy things. The space is what you're after. The thing to get there is just not that important. You can get there much more simply.

R: The reason why it appears difficult to arrive at the space, seems to me to be because our enculturation consists of everything *but* that space. We've talked about a moment that people could meditate on or experience. If you're traveling, and you're lucky enough to have a hotel room to stay in, say you open the door and go in, there's an almost automatic and involuntary turning on of the television in order to crowd out that space, that stillness

We've learned to fear the space, to fear any stillness, any moment of pure silence, because for whatever reason our culture has based itself on the negation of that, right? Not that, not that, not that! What we're really feeling when we feel that fear of that or when we think of that as the void, is our enculturation process speaking. If we can just stay with it, open the door, feel the silence that is there, and not immediately go and turn on the television or immediately attempt to fill that silence with something, that's when it begins to grow.

G: One of the cell phone companies had an ad back in 2001, saying: "Silence is weird." (*laughs*)

R: (*laughs*) But a good kind of weird.

G: But a good kind of weird. People are often afraid. It's part of the fear that so many of us have which prevents us from looking at "no thoughts", because we're just afraid of that space. We don't have any sense it could be anything desirable, pleasurable, interesting, whatever—but that turns out to be false, completely false.

Attachment and suffering

R: Chanting[3] helps me cut through whatever is blocking me, whatever is making me attach. What's beautiful about chanting, even a chant that I've done thousands of times, is that it makes evident where these moments of attachment are. Even if you watch your thoughts a good deal, almost by definition there are little lurkers in there... (*laughs*)

G: (*laughs*)

R: ... that know right where to go exactly when you're —"Oh, he's looking at his thoughts! Into the corner!" Right? And chanting...

G: Lures them out.

R: It really does. It brings them out, and then they announce themselves through blockage of the chant. I know you've gotten a lot of questions about attachment: the nature of attachment, how to work with attachment, is there a problem with attachment? To me, one of the places to start is that attachment which blocks chanting, that you can feel attachment in the experience of chanting.

To me what's important is to start with the feeling of attachment rather than immediately enter into the kind of argumentative or discursive space about defining attachment, whether attachment's a good thing or bad thing, whether we can get rid of it, whether we can't get rid of it, and to just experience it and be with it.

3. See endnote, p.232, *Chanting for non-dual awakening.*

Once we are with it, then we're reminded that we're constantly getting instruction by our own practice or by the cosmos that, "Ooooh there's a little bit over here" that you need to work with, you need to be with. What is that? Don't judge it necessarily right away, don't reject it necessarily right away, but just be with it.

To me that's the beginning of working with attachment, rather than on this semantic level where you say, "Attachment! Attachment is very bad! I need to get rid of attachment. Okay, am I done with attachment now?" One of two things probably happens in my experience; you become attached to the lack of attachment, or, which is the more usual thing, you decide that in fact some attachments are a good thing and that you can only be human, or creative, or fully present, with attachment. I wonder if that resonates with your own experience.

G: Yes, but not everybody chants of course. This is a great vehicle—we do a lot of chanting and it's a great vehicle for what we do. We often chant *Nirvana Shatakam* (see endnote) There's going to be a video up on that as well. It's a great way to categorize things to go after and look for attachment. But I think you make a key point people miss; they think attachment's an intellectual exercise, that you can somehow mentally work your way through it. For me it's a very tactile thing.

Take some example, like a car or something that you're attached to… you know if it were gone you would feel not so cool about it. Try to grok that feeling. Just say "Okay I have this car or bicycle… I'm attached to this bicycle. I know I am because if it went away I'd feel really bad," and then explore the physical feeling of what that sensation is. See if you can feel the clinging in your body from this attachment to this bicycle or car or whatever. You can sit, get into that space and just feel that attachment and say, "Well, this is interesting, because I look at the background, and I look at how I feel differently when I bring the bicycle or the car into consciousness and I feel the energy change in my body." For me that's where you can really get right up close and personal with attachment, not in a merely intellectual way.

R: Yes, I agree entirely. It's this feeling your way through it—that is the way. When you feel it, what you feel is that in that clinging, or grasping, after the object or the person, in fact you're not actually being *with* the bicycle or the car or the person, right?

So the good news is that you can enjoy the bicycle, the person or the car truly by working through and with the attachment, as opposed to just blocking the flow of your relationship. That kind of blocking creates the very clinging that we are concerned with—it's not a good feeling!

G: Absolutely. That's a critical distinction—the attachment really doesn't help us. If we're attached to our partner, we aren't fully present for them. We think, "Attachment's great... if I wasn't attached to him or her, then I wouldn't show I love them."

R: I wouldn't cook dinner for them.

G: You wouldn't cook dinner for them or whatever you were going to do. In fact you find exactly the opposite, that because you are attached to them, then you're up here (in your head) all the time and you're not really clearly experiencing them. So, you let go of the attachment, not the thing itself. This isn't taking your car, bicycle, girlfriend or boyfriend and just pushing them away.

R: Not like just straight off the Rock of Gibraltar into the Mediterranean... (*laughs*)

G: No! (*laughs*) It's not that simple. People have tried that forever—renunciation, detachment, just get rid of the thing. But then you're in your head and you're still deeply attached to it even though it's gone from you; you've not let go of your attachment. It can be there conversely and you'd not be attached to it. It's not getting rid of the thing, it's getting rid of the feeling, the whole hanging on, clinging onto the thing.

R: Right, because the grasping or the clinging to the partner or the spouse, is really the attachment to your map for who that person is—your map, not what they actually are. You ask yourself, "Why isn't that person sticking with my map?" You're not actually even attached to the person.

G: No.

R: You're attached to your own perspective of the person and the conflict (inner and outer) is because they won't cooperate with your perspective of them.

G: They're supposed to behave! (*laughs*)

R: It's, "Look, we've been over this a thousand times. This is how you are, this is how I am." Now the interesting thing is, in my experience, as you let go of attachments, you start to realize that you weren't who you thought you were either. Probably for most of us it's difficult to take this in immediately, except for a little bit at a time, to absorb that our own map of ourselves is a form of attachment.

We're attached to the "I" as we understand it, rather than this field of awareness which we are. By releasing our attachment to some particular preconceived map of the bike, the car, the person and so forth, we actually experience them somewhat more deeply—the person, the bike, the car, the garden—right? In doing that, we release our own fixed identity, our concept of ourselves. By releasing ourselves from our attachment to other things, we paradoxically release ourselves from our attachment to ourselves.

I understand why the language of "liberation" is used for that, because the cessation of a very bad feeling is itself a good feeling. Say I'm really attached to my folding bicycle that I was given for my birthday. If I am present with that, I'd think, "Well it's a beautiful thing that's come into my existence", but I don't feel the importance of it being a continued existence. I only feel the importance of being open to its existence in my life; I don't feel the existence of my securing that in my life.

Attachment has a lot to do with this desire for securing x, y and z in our life. That's an impossible project. You can't secure that within a life of constant change.

G: No, but you have to realize it's impossible. On the other point: you were talking about mapping, and Jiddu Krishnamurti used to say that you could only see yourself through relationship. We have our internal maps of people, and so we have expectations for how they will behave and how they will respond to what we do—what our buttons are that are pushing back and forth. If you're not in any kind of relationship with anything, then you aren't mapping yourself, you aren't exposing yourself to where you are attached. You can see something come into your life, you can watch yourself getting attached to it and you can see the changes happening in you because this thing is here and now.

You can feel underneath that, "What if this thing weren't there? Would I be okay, would I be cool with that?" If you'd say, "No, grumble, grumble, grumble" then that's what you've got to work on. You can see that you've overlaid a map of your own making onto this object/person/thing. I've mapped onto that, some expectation for how it will be forever in my life some way, and how much happier I'll be if I have that. In fact, as you said, that attachment actually blocks your ability to be fully enjoying it because you're so worried about what if she or he leaves me? What if my bike gets stolen?

R: Flat tire!

G: Flat tire! "Whoa, it's got a flat tire! What's wrong with it?" You can really see yourself clearly that way. We get back to the whole thing about suffering and attachment. You really do suffer more, the more you are attached, not because Buddha said that, but because you can watch it in your own life. The more you're attached to something, the more you're afraid of losing it, the more you suffer if it goes away or doesn't conform to our map.

R: Right. When you dwell with, or abide in, that feeling, you say "Oh, well what if that were to go out of my life?" This is where I find self-inquiry very useful. When you say, "Ohhhh, like what if she were gone?" Then you ask, "Who is that, that feels that feeling?" Look, really look, for who it is that feels this need to have that person/place/thing/condition in your life? And you look, and you look, and you look, and you can feel the map dissolving, because the map can't refer to what it's claiming to refer to.

G: Right.

R: There's an implicit map of the "I" that says, "I am the kind of person that absolutely needs that bicycle or else I just don't know what I would do." And you say, "Well who is that 'I'?" That seems to be something that requires repeated practice and intuition to leave the level of words where we just ask who that is, and really use our consciousness to look. If a friend loses an earring in the bathroom, you don't just say "Oh well, you know, maybe it's around here somewhere." (laughs)

G: (laughs)

R: You get down there...

G: You look for it!

R: You don't say, "Oh well, this is the toilet, I better not look in it!" No, you're going to look where the toilet is and you're getting down there to look. "Seek and you shall find", right? It didn't leave the bathroom. It's down there somewhere.

You can say, "Well maybe I'll look, I'm not really interested in who I am, but I'll look and see. Oh look, I'm a Scorpio, on the cusp with Libra!" No! Look—observe.

G: The brain develops a heuristic. If you do that inquiry, "Who am I?, What am I?, What is this?" enough times, the brain develops a heuristic, a rule. It says, "Oh here's a situation." I see the brain feel attachment, and it drops immediately into a feeling. You can feel the brain shifting into "What is this thing that has this attachment?" It happens so quickly and suddenly you can just feel the energy shift. You don't have to sub-vocalize anything, and the thing disappears. It's like magic, the brain gets so adept at this, it just goes bang-bang-bang-bang-bang. The brain can learn how to do it. You just have to do it enough times so that the brain sees that it works, knows how it works, and that's its new program.

R: I can feel people saying, "But the 'I' which is experiencing that is like the pearl in the oyster, you know the sand comes in and then..." or "There's something beautiful about the tragic element of the world, there's something beautiful about suffering. I experience my greatest moments of love experiencing suffering." I think that that is a problem of language: we say these words and we think that they're absolutely fundamental to a full experience, but what they're really pointing to is the—for lack of a better way of putting it—the monistic appreciation of good and evil, of the tragic and the comic, right? What people are afraid they're going to lose if they "lose suffering", which is in a funny way...

G: Yes it is.

R: ... the tragic. But in fact, it's not. You don't suddenly acquire rose-colored glasses and just say "Oh, nothing negative ever happens." What we call negative is an attribute of the One. I see a dead bunny on the road and I really see it more clearly than I would if I were attached and saying,

"Oooh, I'm gonna die! That's me!"

G: Right.

R: I can understand where this desire to hold onto suffering is about authenticity. Perhaps I can be so bold as to suggest that what people really mean when they say that, is that there has to be an appreciation for the tragic element of life, right? The way in which life includes death.

But that only increases as we let go of our attachment because there's no "I" projecting some particular story onto the tragedy or onto the suffering. It actually comes out more in its fullness. You can bear more of the tragic nature of life on planet Earth if you're not attached, than if you are attached, or at least it's my experience.

G: Yes, but there are also people who say, "I love my suffering!" They are strongly attached to their suffering—often unconsciously.

R: Yes, they are.

G: Their suffering is a state they find a paradoxical pleasure in. They're attached to suffering so they haven't made that loop back around to seeing where that's a fundamental problem. If they're hooked into their own suffering as an enjoyable, pleasurable state, and as you just said, try the other thing. Try not being attached to anything and see if your life is richer or not. Let go of your attachment to your suffering and just be open to the flow of the universe. Just be present second by second—things come, things go. See if your life isn't much, much richer than what it was before when you were attached to your suffering.

R: Yes. It's beautiful. Aristotle said that there could be no good story without conflict. What we're really loving when we love our suffering, is the drama. We're loving that we have a story that we can tell about our own unique instance of suffering, and we're probably afraid that if we don't have our suffering, we don't have any story.

G: Who are we? If the story is about me, I'm creating a story because there's the suffering there which reinforces the "I". I'm attached to the suffering so there's an "I" back there holding onto this suffering. The "I" is what's being reinforced. They like drama because it reinforces "me"—"I" get to be center stage. If you go back and de-convolute, deconstruct the "I", you find in fact that you don't need that drama and you aren't attached to your suffering anymore... it just falls away.

R: Because you're not the stage, you're everything.

G: Yes, you're everything! So you can let go of all that suffering and attachment.

R: Yes, I would really encourage, as you did a moment ago, the bringing in of an experimental point of view. Saying "Okay fine, that's one hypothesis, that without suffering you can't have a true authentic existence". That's a hypothesis. Now try this hypothesis. That's the suffering talking, that's your "I" talking and that's your addiction to the "I" talking. Try this.

G: Try this, and just see. You just do it. You will find the right choice. Whatever choice there is for you, try them both. Try A and try B. See if B is not better than A. I found out B is better than A.

R: Then maybe we can stop arguing about it. (*laughs*)

G: (*laughs*) Maybe.

Can inward revolution change sustainability?

R: I somehow intuited this very early on, that we're living in a moment of crisis in our ecosystem. I remember reading when I was about twelve years old that if present trends continued, by the year two thousand there'd be no plants in Japan, which alarmed me at the time of course, but that turned out to be greatly exaggerated. This doesn't mean of course that we don't take these things seriously, but it does mean that we might move beyond our initial panic and wonder what the best approach is to something like sustainability.

I went through a long period where I was looking for solutions to the problem of sustainability in the external world, by redirecting consumer behavior, by finding it in technology, looking at systemic levels. All of those things have merit, but a little further on it seems to me that the way forward in sustainability is really this inward revolution, where, paradoxically, we have to not concern ourselves immediately with a story of success about how sustainable we are or aren't. Instead, let's solve our inner issues which then will manifest its way out through the system. I don't think there are many ears for that right now, out in the world. What's your take on it?

G: Right, yes. Fundamentally we are the consuming creatures that we are because we have a lot of egoic drives, desires, wants and perceived needs that drive all kinds of irresponsible behaviors, both personal and ecological. I believe that if we could find a way to get rid of our egos, or at least get them down to bite-size, we could behave much more responsibly in terms of our planet's ecology, just because we aren't so driven by this big ego. To me, if we want a fundamental change in all our behaviors, ecologically and sustainability-wise, as well as everything else, we've got to somehow go after this egoic construct that's driving all of our needs and desires. If we don't have those, or they are less extreme, then we behave in a wholly different manner.

R: From the perspective of ego, desire feels infinite, personal desire feels infinite, precisely because we're squeezing primary consciousness, the totality of the evolutionary inheritance of our brain, through this tiny little nozzle. If we want something, it feels very big in proportion. It feels as if we're wired for that and we just want that. Many of us have come to believe that we're wired to want to consume more and more and more, but experientially that doesn't seem to be the case. Once the egoic investment withers, it's not that those kinds of consumer desires don't pop up, but they're not the sort of overwhelming life-orienting phenomena that they seem to be otherwise.

G: Exactly! You don't have to find the best gourmet food in the world. You don't have to go around the world trying to find the absolute best and fanciest. You might be just satisfied with having something much simpler. So much of that's driven by our need for moving up and trying to get more and trying to gain status, ego and structure. In fact, if you can pull that—peel that down, that doesn't happen at all, that's not a motivator whatsoever. It becomes less relative and more absolute. So much of our behavior is relative behavior; we see these people getting upset because they only made—one fellow on Wall Street—forty-five million dollars last year.

R: Must be difficult.

G: He said, "I'm quitting my job, this is unacceptable, I've been humiliated long enough!"

ɔreciates him.

ɔpreciates me! And I am taking four of my bud-
ʇe ten million dollars a year and we're quitting
this, we're going to go someplace where they care about us!"
That's a relative game. You see the relative game amongst the
CEO salaries, amongst the sports figure salaries, rock star salaries… it's a relative game. It's not an absolute game. So if we
get the person out of it that's creating this relativity, you get
to, "Okay, what do you really absolutely need to live on? Do
you need forty-five million dollars a year or can you scrape by
on a million dollars a year?" That's the thing that we've got
to get our heads around and what's driving that behavior—
the relative behavior in all of these comparisons. "I'm here on
the pyramid and he's here on the pyramid and I'm certainly
better than he is so pay me some more money." We've got to
unwind that.

R: It's in the marginal differences that both economics and
ecology work, anyway—marginal and relative. We're looking
at stepping down the marginal increases in order to tune our
system, our global infrastructure, towards less impact on the
biosphere. Not this kind of total renunciation that I think
often sits in the background of a lot of people's understanding
of where we have to go with sustainability—we don't have to
say "no" to a beautiful fulfilling life. Of course not.

In other words, to entertain the argument somebody might
say, "Well if people didn't chase down the absolute best gourmet food all over the world, and they didn't push themselves
to produce the most beautiful effective presentation of it, we
wouldn't have that kind of pursuit of beauty in the world."
But of course, the counter-argument would be, "Well, why
don't you find the beauty that's right in front of you already
instead of chasing it around the world?" That's part of what
people think they hear… they hear sustainability and they
think "less", they hear "boring", maybe they see masses of

Eastern Bloc people queuing for extremely rough toilet paper. When, in fact, it is about beauty, what we're talking about, this inward revolution. It's just about not chasing beauty that is only relative and not absolute.

G: Yes. As you've experienced yourself, as you begin to unwind this egoic structure, you can find beauty in the simplest things. There's so much elegance in a leaf, or frost on the grass, or a flower. Not to get all poetical on this thing but there's great beauty in everyday life by just getting yourself out of the way, getting your relative ideas—"Oh yes, I saw this great painting at the Met yesterday," whatever it was, and you can't just walk outside the Met and walk into Central Park and see that in fact there's fantastic beauty in Central Park that has nothing to do with something costing forty-five million dollars. You can just walk over and see the squirrels, you can see the flowers, you can see the trees, and there's great beauty in that. We've got to get away from believing that it has to be some expensive object and find that really in our daily lives, if you get out of the way, you can move into that space.

R: We have to get away from the idea that simplifying our consumption and simplifying our life somehow means we're living a less aesthetic existence. To the contrary, everything begins to sparkle once you're no longer looking past it to the Met or the Lamborghini or the gourmet food. That's where the feedback loops really start to operate. I learned this at first from taking ecodelics, but then I learned to appreciate it through meditation where just tarrying for a minute with the nature of what actually is can become overwhelmingly beautiful.

G: Austerity can take on a crazy aspect, too. One of the famous teaching stories out of India was that two renunciates (sannyasis) renounced everything. They'd thrown away all their stuff and they were down to just loincloths, and they were sitting on the beach arguing with each other because one guy thought the other guy's loincloth was a little bit too finely woven. (*laughs*)

R: (*laughs*)

G: It really gets down to, you've got to change the person —change the perspective. You can't just change the external surroundings. It's not enough to say that I'm down to my loincloth, or you'll get "Well your loincloth is pretty fancy!"

R: You're getting awfully uppity with your loincloth. (*laughs*)

G: (*laughs*)

R: And it was too fancy!

G: (*laughs*) It really does get down to you've got to get the person out of it, you've got to get the egoic structure out of it, because no matter how much you give away, you can still be sitting there with just a loincloth on the beach and you'll be comparing! So the issue is getting that egoic structure broken down so it doesn't run after structured, relative achievements.

R: I think it was Gandhi, when people asked him, "How is it that I can have possessions or you can have possessions?" And he said, "Possessions are no problem whatsoever. Renounce the possessor."

G: That's right, exactly, yes.

R: So, to loop it back to sustainability, is it fair to offer the apparent non sequitur which is that if you care about sustainability, if you care about the eco systemic destiny of the planet, if you care about biodiversity, you should meditate?

G: Yes, we've touched on this. If you realize it's all one and not just metaphorically, or philosophically or intellectually, if you really do begin to understand that this is all one thing, not just me and the rest of the things, then why would you go around doing what you do? You just say, "Oh. This is all one thing. Why would I mess this up?" and you behave differently. But you've got to somehow unwind that structure in a way that gives you that clear, true understanding that includes, but isn't limited to, the intellectual aspect.

R: Some people recognize "it's all one thing" in a conceptual way. Others are allergic to it in an equally conceptual way because they equate it with monotheism or fascism or... I've found it useful to ask myself, "Where does it start? If there are separate things, where do they begin and end, where is the boundary between one thing and another thing?" The closer I look at any allegedly separate thing, such as myself or another person, I find that it's not separate. That could be one path of inquiry that people would take up, to ask themselves "Where could there possibly be anything else... since it's all one thing."

G: Right, right.

DIY non-dual awakening

R: You're an experimentalist by background?

G: Empirical scientist by training.

R: Right. It was material science?

G: Yes. The point being that we've come at this awakening thing as cleanly, as sparsely and empirically as we can. The idea was to say, "Could we just strip all the philosophy out, all the teachings, no magic books, no teachers, just have experiments you could just run yourself and just try them out?"

R: Right.

G: See how far you can get.

R: That's what was attractive to me because I come from a background in philosophy; I had looked at all of the different traditions and I was starting to find some persistent patterns that I was interested in, but the way to test those patterns is by having arguments with other philosophers...

G: Yes, who the best arguer is!

R: Oh, I am, yes! (*laughs*)

G: (*laughs*)

R: There's something very unsatisfying about that. You can win a philosophical argument and lose the game entirely. The game is to investigate the actual nature of mind and the way in which we change our experience of mind, so this experimental practice that I've learned in part from you is really fundamental. It means that there's no teaching really, there's nothing that you do just because it says so in a book, even though it's nice that there are books that seem to resonate with what it is we're saying. There's no one practice that definitely is definitively the way...

G: Right.

R: There is no way anybody else can ever tell you what your own practice is. All they can do is guide you to practices that have worked for them. As is the case with every other experiment that is worthy of a name, they have to be repeatable. It won't do to just have a kind of one-off experience: "Oh, yes I've experienced pure consciousness."

G: You said something that was really important too... this is basically a DIY, do-it-yourself, so you need a feedback mechanism. The useful thing about this practice, is that what you focus on is this self-referential internal narrative. It goes on all the time in almost everybody's brain, so you've got a ready-at-hand, inexpensive (actually free) feedback tool to see if in fact your experiment's working. You try the experiment, you look... "Has it changed? Is it less energetic? Is it more problematic? No. Has it modified at all? Have I lost any kind of a number of thoughts per hour or anything?" You've got your automatic DIY feedback.

It's also important to make sure that it was from contemporary people; people who have been alive while we've been alive. So you can say, "Okay, this is not passed down through 2,500 years, passed down through four languages, and god knows how many revisionists to get to me today." You can look at videos of these people, see pictures of them, you can meet them and actually talk to them. So it's not that you have to rely on any hope that you're getting the right version of what was said, you know exactly what was said.

R: Right, it's not true just because it's old.

G: No! No, on the contrary, is it true because it's new? How come nobody thought of it before? So, it does push you right into the moment of yes, we can experiment with this thing, believing you can find this way by no teachings, no philosophies, just by your own experiments.

R: When you use the word "experiment" and "your mind" in the same sentence...

G: Yes.

R: ... it can sound frightening. It may be worth talking about, what people can expect to be in for.

G: Well, and I think you touched on it. The important thing is recognizing that this may not be a uniformly smooth journey. You've got a brain with 100 billion neurons and 100 trillion synaptic interconnections—some parts of those are going to be reorganized somewhat and they aren't going to come out uniformly. You may see a network start to become no longer valuable, and the brain then changes its purpose, repurposes that circuit. As it does, you may get a shot of some old memories, some old fear that you had, and you didn't know this, so it will be bumpy, progress can be made. It will not be uniformly smooth.

R: Then the first protocol for the experimental method needs to be first of all, become aware that there are fish in the aquarium as it were...

G: Ah yes, fish in the aquarium.

R: Become aware by observing your own thoughts, that there is that inner narrative there. Then look at the suite of techniques that are available to dwindle that inner narrative. Check and see if those techniques are affecting the inner narrative. If yes, proceed. If no, try a different technique or try more often or...

G: Right. Yes, I think it's important that you just hit on "many techniques". What everybody finds is that the "I", this I-ego that you're trying look at and inquire about and see what its nature is, is very clever and crafty. It wants to stick around and keep its job, so you might try one approach and you find in fact that it can't go any further. It's found a way to blunt that, so you've got to sneak around some other way and come in with another, maybe similar, but different, approach and it'll be able to make an incursion into the structure of the "I" before the "I" can run around and block it off. Eventually you'll have put enough incursions into the "I" that in fact it won't be able to reconstruct itself enough to persist.

R: Right. So, for example, in realizing that the "I" is a fictional construct, sometimes it can feel as though, "Wow, I am the creator of my own experience. I'm the director. I'm the play-wright. I'm the producer." That can feel both at once very tempting and also very awful in its level of responsibility, like you have this responsibility to be who you are. I personally found that it was important to have that fictional character surrender to something much larger than itself, whatever we want to think of that larger entity being. The important thing was that the larger entity was compelling enough that I could surrender that fictional construct, otherwise you get stuck at that level of fictional construct.

G: Yes, the part to the realization is that there may be some-thing there, and you come into it by degrees. But you begin, you start the surrendering process and you say, "Ohhh, this is dangerous!", and you find out that it wasn't dangerous at all. I surrendered this little thing, and it wasn't a problem… that's okay. You just work your way incrementally into more and more surrendering. You find that the more you let go, somehow—and this gets woo-woo—somehow there's a strong sense of support, there's a strong sense of okay-ness about the surrendering process that's not dangerous. Nothing bad is happening to you because of this and it feels good as you surrender. Actually some neurotransmitters get released and you begin to see things loosening up. So it is supported by the brain and by the neurochemistry, but you do it incrementally.

R: Maybe the reason why that occurs that way is that when we surrender we're really not surrendering anything but our consciousness concerning something...

G: It's a construct we have.

R: Exactly.

G: A story, a memory...

R: Right. So it's not like I am giving up my job. No. I am giving up my attachment to the job. The consciousness of my job can't possibly be dangerous except insofar as I'm holding onto it.

G: That's right.

R: Right. So what's dangerous about it is not that all of a sudden I'm going to give away all my stuff to some guru or something. On the contrary, what's going to happen is that I'm going to release all these things that are feeding my inner narrative. One way to think about why it feels like there's something there is the more we release and let go the more we're actually in pure consciousness. The less we're filling pure consciousness with the equivalent of junk food content and the more time we spend in pure consciousness, the more at home we feel. It feels like we're at home.

G: It has to be that way or it wouldn't work. If this was such a horrible, unusual strange place, this wouldn't work. It turns out that's what you feel as you aptly described... it begins to open up and it does feel like home. It does feel like you're returning home. You're not going to a strange place, you're coming back home again. It feels like such a sweet thing, you think, "This isn't going to be dangerous. I was afraid of this place but I find I'm just going back home again." You feel more and more valid and more and more integrated. You become as one thing, piece by piece, so you end up getting more holistic all the time.

R: Right, and you start to see the way in which all the parts of your life that you thought you were orchestrating or failing to orchestrate were really just coming into being and just passing...

G: Passing through.

R: ... passing through, and in pure consciousness you can sort of hang out and be part of the adventure without getting caught up in the adventure in the same way that you did before.

G: The important distinction that you made was that it's attachment to things that's the problem not the things themselves. There's nothing wrong with your car—but if you're heavily attached to it, you will suffer...

R: Yes.

G: ... because of the attachment to that car.

R: Yes, you just got something on it... there's some dust on it!

G: (*laughs*) A bird!

R: Stand away from the car!

G: Don't scratch the car...

R: I've got to kill all birds! Otherwise...

G: Exactly, and the same thing with your relationships. You don't push the people away, you just recognize that in fact you may be deeply attached and it's probably constraining your ability to be fresh and new in that relationship. So you're only seeing it through the eyes of the story that you're maintaining about this relationship. What we're saying is that if you can get out of the way, a whole new kind of relationship can take place because you aren't running under that old model.

R: Right. So you can experiment your way into an entirely new life.

G: Exactly, exactly, yes… absolutely.

R: Now it can be helpful, I have found, to be able to be in dialogue with other people that are engaged in this.

G: Right.

R: But again, another protocol needs to be, that nobody else really knows what anybody else…

G: … is really thinking.

R: … is going through.

G: No, you really don't. It's really your personal subjective thing and the most you can do is kind of triangulate on what the rose smells like. It smells like this, but not like that, and tastes like this, but not like that. So you're just helping them try to flesh out the idea for themselves as well as try to communicate to you and see if it can be validated at some level, although it can't be completely and externally validated—ever.

R: Right, except for by the Self.

G: Yes, by yourself, you're self-validated.

R: But there are definitely patterns and pitfalls. I find that I'm able to learn from other people having gone along this path. I find that by saying "Oh yes, when I realized that I'd given up everything, that I'd surrendered everything except for those things that were really the closest to me like my family and my job, that was the most difficult point. But I was also able to see that what I was really surrendering was neither of those things... only my consciousness of those things, my attachment to those things."

G: As you begin the surrendering process, say for your job or something, you can see how your job changes. The way you go into your job changes as you surrender even little pieces of it, so you become more effective in your job. So you say, "This is a good process, I'm not losing my job, my salary's not going down, I'm functioning better at the workplace. There's not as much fight, not as much conflict, I work in meetings better, and I'm more present for the meetings." It gets better very quickly.

R: It really does. There is an initial period where the experimentalist has to be persistent and even, just try again, even if it gets bumpy, but there's definitely a very rapid return on breaking even a little bit with any of your stories about any of your most cherished attachments.

G: Yes. You know I think the only faith it takes is just to say, "I'll try this experiment."

R: That's it.

G: You know I've got this experimental book, "I'll just run the experiment and see if it works or not." No more than that. When you do, then things start to happen to reinforce that very quickly.

R: (*Agrees*) Experiment on.

G: Experiment on.

Does the world need to be "fixed" or is it "perfect"?

R: This morning it was occurring to me that one of the most important practices is to experiment at least with the idea that everything is absolutely and totally perfect. This came out of nowhere for me on my own path because, what could be more obvious than the fact that of course, everything is totally and completely fracked up, right? As my wife put this this morning, "Don't we have enough things to worry about?" (*laughs*)

G: (*laughs*)

R: It's very counterintuitive. It cuts across left, right, all religious affiliations… the world is something that needs to be fixed. One of the things that might be good to share is this at least experimental approach to the idea that everything is totally and completely perfect.

G: You say experimental.

R: Yes.

G: What do you mean?

R: Well, one of the things that seems to happen if you say to somebody, "You know everything is completely perfect." (*laughs*)

G: (*laughs*) … once they stop laughing!

R: Yes, exactly! Well, after they say, "Perfect… okay, is this perfect?"

G: Yes, how perfect is this?

R: There's just such an enormous resistance towards automatically accepting that it's perfect. It's very closely related, if not identical, to the 'no free will' discussion that we have had.

G: Ah, yes, it is indeed.

R: If you say right away, "You know, you're not in control. Just let go of that," that is too much for most people to really tolerate at first, it's like too big of a dosage in some ways. Whereas if you say, "Next time you feel frustrated, experiment with the idea that you can surrender and experience the fact that you're not in control," that's what I mean by experiment. We can experiment with the idea that most of my life I've been waking up in the morning and most of my day operating according to the principle of, "and this thing needs to be fixed, and that thing needs to be fixed." The business model of businesses, religions, institutions of all kinds, is built on this idea. "Let us fix that for you! There's something wrong." If you come on too powerfully all at once and say, "Everything is perfect, get over it," nobody's going to have ears for that, nobody's going to really incorporate and integrate that. But if you say, "This is a really interesting experimental protocol…" You can listen to somebody who has tried it, and say "This is really interesting. Try this little script that everything is perfect."

G: Yes. Like everybody else, I felt I was responsible for fixing the world. You don't look at that and consider the absolute arrogance of that assumption; there are 7 billion people on the planet and the Universe, whatever that is, has been sitting around on Her hands waiting for you to come along and fix the whole thing.

So you can start getting into asking "Okay, who is it that believes they are responsible for fixing this or has the ability to do so?" Just ask, "Who is it that feels they're going to be in charge of fixing the world?" See if in fact that's reasonable, credible? I backed into all this just by doing inquiry... "Who am I, where am I, what is this?"

Eventually, as that whole thing fell away when the "I" fell away, there's no one there to run around and do something. There is no one who has this long term vision of how to fix the world. Along with that came, as you pointed out, no free will, because there was no one to have free will and no one to be in control. There was just no one to suffer, no one to have fears, and no one to have self-referential desires. The whole thing just fell apart like a house of cards.

When you say, "I'm going to fix the world" try not going out into the object of 'fixing the world'. If you go online, you can spend 83 hours today looking at all the problems the world has, or you can take a few minutes and look back in and ask who is it that believes they're going to be fixer of the world? Just feel into the "I" of that "I'm going to fix the world." Go back into "I". What does it feel like now?

If you get into that space of "What is this that's looking at this presumption?"... Just feel that space... and you've done that. You feel there's nothing wrong with this space. This space looks like it's already perfect, there's nothing I could change in this space. Then something comes in, pulls you away and you're off on fixing the world again. But you've had a little glimpse of something that really is perfect, where you can't find anything that needs to be done to it to make it any better.

R: When you're in that space which is not the Source, when you're a doer who is going about fixing the world, almost inevitably you're missing out on something—and that something is loving the world. You're not experiencing the world as world. You're experiencing the world as a doer who is separate from the world and is then going to get in there and fix the world. It feels like the reason why this could be a good experimental protocol to follow, if you can just say "Yeah, it's perfect!" Then that allows you to be in the world. When you are in the world, that turning around and looking at the one who is in the world feels to me a little bit easier. It feels like it's less clenched.

When the world seems like nothing but an ensemble of existential threats, then the ego and the narrative mind are very good at saying, "Well that's all well and good, but the tiger's at the edge of the village! In fact the village is surrounded by cyborg tigers!" Right? Then it feels—mistakenly—like there's no space to get still and turn around and see it, and so the suffering then just continues. Whereas if I experiment with "Wow it's really perfect!" I can experience in that moment, as a moment, just a little bit of that space where nothing needs to be gained and nothing is lost.

G: Right. The key to seeing it, too, is to watch where you are in your head, what your consciousness is doing. If you're really present for *now*—not in a cliché like "be here now", but if you really are no place else mentally in your consciousness, there's nothing else pulling you off into the past, into the future, you're just here… You can feel when you pull, when you move out of that towards "doing" something, it's "Whoa, this is not cool!" It feels so different from this being in the Source, which is such a sweet place. It's "Whoa, this is not cool!"

The most perfect place you find is to be in that Presence because it is so compelling. The brain finds out that it likes this—we've talked before about this… And the brain will re-functionalize itself to support this. The brain is after as much pleasure and as little pain as possible. This is the best deal in town, so it will go there. The more time you spend there, the more it really becomes "home". Coming out of that becomes "not okay." It is perfect, at least the best you can find, and nothing else you can do is going to make it feel so good.

R: This is why dialogue is so vital because, speaking out of my own experience, when I would pull away or drop out of the feeling of the Source, very often I would look to something in the world to get me back there.

G: What would that 'something' be?

R: Yes, exactly! And then that wouldn't work, so I'd try another one. Whereas what's so interesting is that if you can, on a regular basis, enter into dialogue with someone else who is also in Source, it's like you become two mutually-corrective mechanisms. You feel yourself falling out of Source and then the other person more or less feels this and sort of directs you back to Source gently. Then you feel it again. It seems to have to happen I don't know how many times!

G: (*laughs*)

R: It's a really beautiful experience. What's comes out of it, as we've discussed, is one of the reasons why it doesn't make any sense for teaching to cost any money if it doesn't need to, because this kind of dialogue is its own reward: as you fall away from the Source, the other helps bring you back to the Source. As they bring you back to the Source, you help bringing them back to the Source because even their bringing you back to the Source, can be a little bit of a separating ordeal.

G: As you found out, as you work with people, and if you work from Source, you find that you get deeper and deeper. If you're staying in Source, then if you're working with somebody, you are at some level pulled into Source even more deeply because you're trying to come out of this and express what you feel towards this person. Source is also in them, you don't have a special copy. They also have it.

So the deeper you sink into it, the more likely they are able to become coherent with you—and this gets kind of woo-woo now. There is some kind of wavelength coherence between the two of you, and so both of you become more deeply immersed into Source and less likely to be pulled out. That's where the perfection comes—when the two of you are in coherence, congruence, and there's just no place else you'd rather be, no place else to go, nothing else to get, nothing else to bring in, nothing else to take out... it's perfect. If you can let that be the experience between both of you, then the whole thing really takes on a great richness, and it is perfect.

R: This addresses also another common rejoinder to the idea that everything is perfect, which is, "Well you're just living in your own world. I'm sure it seems perfect to you if you've managed to blot out the reality of a world with... "

G: That you're "bypassing".

R: "... 6 billion people on the brink... ", you know, and so on. The contrary is the case. It's precisely by doing something besides living in my own world which is fed by this "the world is broken, I need to do something about that", that sense of separation. You start to feel the perfection, and the perfection starts to manifest more and more. We get to see that this planet that we live on is just an incredible unfolding of perfection, and insofar as we would ever dare to say that it's not perfect, it's precisely the effect of our not recognizing its perfection that is fracking it up, right?

G: As you remain in Source or in Presence or Stillness or whatever word you want to use, you find that the actions that manifest are much more prescient, organic and holistic than your fragmented mind's going to come up with. You can feel yourself moving out of Source into fragmentation, and as you do, you can see the quality of your actions going down precipitously. They just immediately start to fall off.

We talked about how fast the feedback is when you come out of Source. You can watch yourself going through your day and it's like, "Whoa, slap on the face, bang... " and you're back into Source again. You can see very quickly how suboptimal you become and how fast it occurs. The slightest nudge and you're out of Source. You (*ksshhht*) get back in again.

R: So when it comes to, say, questions of politics which is the level at which we would start to organize and manipulate the world so that it can be fixed, because of that premise that the world needs to be fixed, maybe a good heuristic is: does this political activity keep me in Source? Or does it pull me out of Source? If it helps keep me in Source, fantastic. If it pulls me out of Source shouldn't we watch, at least observe and witness, whether or not the goals are being served by politics?

I'm not arguing against politics, I've just noticed that a lot of times people make the move from "the world needs to be fixed, and here's how, and I along with a lot of other I's are gonna act on that." How many dry runs of that, how many case studies do we need to see, as people have been talking about fixing the world for two thousand years? If you look closely at any of these attempts to fix the world they've done the opposite.

Dysfunctional evolution of the mind

G: There is no "blah, blah" going on in a chimpanzee's mind, according to current levels of knowledge. As far as we know those very nearest, almost genetically identical primates to us, chimpanzees, do not have a constructed, conceptual language in the way that we do, which makes it probable that, unlike us, they don't have the "blah, blah" going on in their minds like so many of us humans do. That doesn't mean they don't have symbolic images passing through, but the constant "blah blah" is kind of a human-special "disease" as nearly as we can tell.

E: The ego.

G: The ego. This ego that we create is a human-special disease, and it may be because we've become so highly socialized.[4] You will never see two chimpanzees carrying one log. They just do not cooperate that way. Although they have a complex range of interactions they almost never cooperate as a group to do anything large, and no other primates, almost no other animals, make enormous organizational structures to accomplish bigger goals. Humans are unique in that. Our cerebral cortex is specialized for social relationships. So we're unique, maybe uniquely cursed, whatever word you want to use for this, because we have this very active ego going on.

   Is this a modern disease or not? Some people say so. We supposedly have fifty-five thousand thoughts a day. So as

---

4. Social insects work together precisely because there is no separation into individuals. Cf E.O. Wilson. They are unique, sentient, but not egoic. This holds for plants as well.

our world has gotten more complex, it's possible that we are thinking a lot more. We are doing a lot more internal processing, a lot more "blah, blah" is going on. We have so much information coming at us now, so much data, and our world is so much more complex than it was, say 500 years ago, that we're thinking about all this stuff and we're doing fifty-five thousand thoughts a day. That surely can't be necessary.

R: For example, I always sort of choked on the idea that there was more information now bombarding us than there was in the past because, if you go to the Amazonian rainforest, there's an enormous information flow in that rainforest. What's distinctive and has kind of led to this runaway process in part, is that we're now being bombarded with all this information that is seemingly directed at us. It's, "Hey you! Hey you! Hey you! Hey you!" Whereas the information gradients in the Amazonian rainforest, there's kind of a differential... it's not about us, it's not directed at us.

We can create mythologies where it is about us, but we almost can't escape the myth that it's about us now. What's interesting is, is that if you think about this, you think about another forest or another garden and you look at the Old Testament, at Genesis... The tale of Adam and Eve and Eve's eating of the fruit of the tree of knowledge of good and evil is exactly the false story that we're talking about. Both the freedom and the burden of being able to have an ego are allegorically represented in the second and third book of Genesis—the freedom and the burden of making judgments, of deciding between pros and cons. In the context of the allegory, a garden is intentionally made for these human beings and they do what you would expect them to do in that garden—which is eat everything within the garden. As a result, we get the gift of awareness, the scales fall from our eyes or we become aware that we're naked.

But then we have to make the next move. It's almost like

we've been in that part of the drama since the second and third book of Genesis, and we haven't made it to the next point so that we can look back to see where that capacity to make these alleged judgments came from. In fact Eve wasn't making the judgment at all: she was *meant* to eat the fruit, if you read the book of Genesis. It's really interesting that we've been aware of this problem for a really long time, even if it has probably metastasized in modernity. It gets imprinted into the stories that we tell ourselves. It's kind of unavoidable. No matter how much we try to dodge the fact of the present moment and the fact that the present moment offers the fourth state of consciousness[5] that is beyond this egoic calculating state of consciousness, it persists. It cannot be defeated as it were.

I feel, in that sense, very optimistic that we can maybe continue this evolutionary move from the chimp, which is in some ways perfectly tuned to its own environment without the egoic rider pretending to bond over characters. Then we humans come along, and for seventy thousand years occupy this kind of dream world of imagining each other being the characters. Now we're at the next phase where we can know that's what we're doing and look back and activate that other part of our consciousness which is not excluded by the egoic consciousness. However much the egoic consciousness thinks that it can exclude that fourth state of consciousness, it cannot.

G: Yes, I think it's important to look at this as the next step of evolution, not a step back to what a chimpanzee has which is no symbolic consciousness, no "blah, blah" going on as nearly as we can tell. The question is, are we de-evolving, are we taking a Copernican demotion to move back to "chimpanzee mind" or are we trying to take the next step ahead? I think the argument is, we're making the next step ahead, that we

---

5. The fourth state of consciousness or *Turiya* is that which underlies the other states of waking, dreaming and deep sleep. It is what never changes and in which all states, concepts and beliefs are subsumed.

want to be able to use symbolic consciousness[6] to problem-solve, plan, etc. That appears to be unimpeded even as we shut down largely this selfing, this "blah, blah" network that's very egoically-focused. The idea is that we can move forward.

We're at a tipping point. If you look around, things are not going very well right now. I do think our timespan to do something about it, is finite and not long. We need something to change our perspective—like it must have been when it was first recognized that the earth is not the center of the universe and that the earth is not flat. Some kind of a change in our ego construction so that we can live responsibly in this world with each other, act more humanely, share better, all of the things we don't do well now because we have this overactive ego now with fifty-five thousand thoughts a day. How can we get coherent policy out of somebody whose mind's running fifty-five thousand thoughts a day?

R: And probably more. The average policy analyst is probably a hundred and fifty thousand.

G: (*laughs*)

E: An artificial intelligence that does ethics, that's where I think we're going—honestly.

G: If we're going to abrogate our responsibility, it will still leave us behind though with then maybe seventy thousand thoughts a day and completely miserable. So, can we evolve ourselves? We're just an eye blink evolutionarily now. Twitter's been around for five years and Facebook eight years which is a very short timeframe against millions of years of evolution and seventy thousand years of symbolic consciousness. We've got to be very perceptive and very proactive in doing something

---

6. Symbolic consciousness is consciousness that uses symbols to represent elements in both the outer world and inner world to facilitate language, communication, and reasoning about those elements.

or we're going to run out of resources, we're going to run out of life, this is going to be a nasty place. We have to somehow recognize this is a critical time, we have to do something.

R: One of the ways that a runaway process can be instigated is that the very thing that we all appear to be chasing as globalization, takes more and more people into the orbit of consumer capitalism and modernity is right here in us. It's been wrapped in religious garb. It's been wrapped in a kind of spiritual message. But I think there's a way of understanding it.

We all have this kind of bliss, as our birthright. While it was useful in an evolutionary sense to chase it for a while, it's long since outstripped its usefulness in terms of chasing more and more goods and services that get distributed over the planet. There's two billion people that we don't really pay any attention to who don't have electricity or clean water and so forth.

Again I feel optimistic because that bliss is a very powerful input into the system. So even if we have a finite period of time, which I obviously agree with, and even if we're facing some version of total planetary distress, we have a very powerful technology in that fight and that technology just happens to be within us.

G: Just imagine a world without an ego. Just imagine if nobody had...

R: (*starts singing* Imagine *by John Lennon*)

G: ... egoic consciousness's that we do now. You might think, "I would behave very badly, I would do awful things if I didn't have an ego protecting me, if I didn't have "blah, blah" helping me... "

R: I would cut in line at the McDonald's. (*laughs*)

G: Yes, exactly! But then, in fact you don't cut in line at McDonald's without an ego.

R: No, because I'm enjoying my bliss.

G: You actually behave better.

R: Yes.

G: There's no record demonstrating the fact that if you lose thoughts you suddenly become some awful person, it just doesn't happen. You are very heavily conditioned, you have genetics, you have epigenetics, you've had cultural conditioning, you've had friends around you, a lot of experiences... you're not going to suddenly run upstairs and throw your chair through the window. It just doesn't happen. You're just not going to behave that way. This never occurs. You just overestimate how important this egoic consciousness is to keeping your behavior in check. It doesn't keep it in check. It's what causes all the problems.

R: Rather like how we overestimate the role of nation states in creating order in human societies. We think "Oh, what would we do without a nation state in order to make sure that we all didn't destroy ourselves?" But in fact, the problem is within each of us, and the solution is within each of us.

G: We believe religions are here to keep us behaving morally, to behave in a respectful and peaceful and loving way. And yet, log on! It's absolutely not the case. It's not just one particular religion, it's many, many... perhaps all religions have the same problem. They really do not free us to be open to whatever our truth is, our Self. They want to give us the story. They want to give us a protocol... even when I have the protocol installed in me right now... you don't need anybody's help for this."

R: Ironically each one of them contains within them the story of that—that the 'kingdom of heaven is within'.

G: At the very top, at the beginning! At the very beginning, that's right.

R: Every single one of them points to this fourth state of consciousness as being something that's available to each and every one of us.

G: But it gets processed down through two thousand, or fifteen hundred or five hundred or two thousand five hundred years. There's a lot of massaging that goes on, and a lot of people involved who are invested in this thing, working…

R: We'll just make a little bit of money off of that for a…

G: Just a little bit. Yes. So you've got to find a way to set people free. This really is about personal freedom, absolute personal freedom. You can be free of that institutional constraint. You can be free of your ego. There's a whole different "you" there that's just ready to go if you can just get out of the way.

Erich: Reminds me of what the Dalai Lama had posted on his Facebook page two weeks ago.

R: Even the Dalai Lama got a dopamine hit with that!

G: What we're talking about now is if you just begin deconstructing the ego then you deconstruct the need for… religion, for an institution to tell me what to do, because I find out that in fact I know what to do. If I just get "blah, blah" out of the way, I'm not constructing an imaginary future. I'm just living right now. I chopped wood and carried water before. I chop wood and carry water now. You just aren't "blah, blah, blah" up here in the head when you're chopping wood and carrying water. Look at how hard the church fought against the proof that the earth wasn't the center of the universe. People had hot pokers jammed through their tongues before they were burned to death because they wouldn't recant their view that the earth is not the center of the solar system, let alone the universe. It's ridiculous, but there's an investment in the status quo that preserves these obscure beliefs, these absolutely unquestionable "just believe this" matters of "faith".

R: Yes, religions exist in order to tell the story of themselves. In that sense they're like self-replicating discourses, and we can actually give thanks to them for that. Like the Dalai Lama, much of Buddhist dharma wouldn't exist if Tibet hadn't been telling the story of Buddhism to itself for the past fifteen hundred years. But, as the Dalai Lama seems to himself recognize, that's not what it's about anymore. Okay, thank you for preserving that and we can actually learn a lot from those stories about how to activate our fourth state of consciousness, how to deactivate our egoic state of consciousness, because that's part of the story they've been telling about themselves. But they neither have a monopoly on that nor are they necessary and sufficient to that. So what's going to be interesting is, is there a way for us to transition to a kind of society that is post-religious but intensely sacred, if I can...

G: Well, it's spiritual versus religious.

R: Yes.

G: That's what we're questioning. I don't see any proclivity on the parts of the churches to disempower themselves. On the contrary, they're trying to maintain their power at all costs despite very bad behaviors in many of the churches. What value do religions have now today? This is not neo-atheism, that's not new Advaita-speak, this is saying, "Let's be spiritual, let's not be religious." "Religious" to me is the very antithesis of what spirituality is about. You've structured something that was alive, and now made it dead, but something that we're fighting to preserve at all costs.

R: One of the greatest hoaxes in history. Something we have to do ourselves gradually gets outsourced to somebody else. That's really the kernel of the message—there's nobody to do it but each and every one of us together. As a friend of mine says, "There's nothing to it but to do it." It's not difficult. It doesn't require a special initiation.

G: We have been disempowered. Our institutions have taken our power away from us. They've told us "You can't do it yourself. You aren't capable of this. We have to tell you what to do." In fact, that's not the case, not in this field.

R: That's what makes this Dalai Lama example a beautiful one, actually. You have a person who is part of a previously theocratic society saying, it can't work.

Yet there's always another level of initiation or achievement that is there within all of these beautiful traditions, that is there to, in some sense, tempt us, almost. You're saying, "Ah well, it's true that all I have to do is turn off my mind and dwell and watch my own thoughts. But you know, maybe if I got the Kalachakra Initiation… that would really be the thing!"

What's interesting about this is that the very difficulty of moving beyond the status quo, beyond the traditions that disempower us, is actually a great gift. It's there to make us work through whatever it is we have to work through. In this case it feels like, those initiations, those levels of achievement and so forth that many of our institutions are fond of and work off of, are there to challenge us to let go of our need for any kind of external verification of our experience whatsoever.

G: We're tuned that way as humans. It's very important to me if the person above me in the hierarchy accepts me, rewards me, promotes me and everything else. Not just Buddhism, but all religions, have structure in them. There are sects within all religions that don't do this, but everybody else has a graded scale. Not surprisingly, with the graded scale, it costs money, it costs performance, it costs dedication to the cause to earn your way up the ladder.

R: The stairway to heaven.

G: The stairway to heaven. That's what got Martin Luther to leave the Catholic Church—the selling of indulgences. You could buy your way into purgatory, you could get Uncle Fred out of purgatory... you could do it all. That's the very nature of who we are as an evolutionarily-derived entity, is that we have this structural hierarchy within us. If someone can come in and say, "Look, I'm the alpha, I'm higher up in this hierarchy than what you are, and I can say you're kind of okay, I can move you up two levels... "

R: Oh, thank you very much!

G: Then we're programmed to respond to that, and we do! And not just in religions, but all organizations have learned this in fact—you can be a faculty member—a level one, a level two, a level three, a level four, a level five, a level six...

R: (*coughs*) Liberal Arts Research Professor...

G: (*laughs*) Yes, exactly! Even in our university, there're so many hierarchical levels that you can get into! Organizations have learned this about us, how we operate, and they can give away a badge of promotion that's worth a lot of money. We'll trade a lot for being called "this" as opposed to being called "that".

R: Actually I have a title that is actually worth no money at all, it's just a title. It's Liberal Arts Research Professor.

G: Isn't that beautiful though? Isn't it great to have it?

R: They've perfected it totally so that it doesn't actually have to mean anything at all.

G: Yes! Anything! It means nothing.

R: It's like those coats of arms that you can get if you go to Ireland and you happen to have something remotely Irish... "Oh here's your coat of arms!" You still get the dopamine shot.

G: Yes, when I was in organizations, that's what you do for a living, that's all we did! "You can be Third Assistant Vice President… "

R: Senior Executive Vice President of Operations.

G: Exactly. So, I've suggested demoting the ego and giving it a different job to do. You just say, "Well you're going to be Second Third Assistant in charge of 'something', later. We're going to promote you, later. But you're not going to be in charge of the place anymore."

R: In fact, nobody's in charge.

G: Nobody's in charge, you aren't going to be in charge, but you'll have a job, and here's your title, a long title, and they go off and do that job. We watch it in ourselves, how we get caught up in promotions and titles and how much people will fight for this much difference in status in large organizations. It's feeding off of how we evolved as our numbers increased and we developed agriculture.

Enlightenment is a process not a goal...

G: How about Harada Roshi's famous statement, "Enlightenment is capable of endless enlargement" which startled so many people? He was a Zen master from the late nineteenth/early twentieth century and was quoted in *The Three Pillars of Zen* by Philip Kapleau.

R: Well you could see that the contrary position has a kind of pedagogical value saying, "Yes enlightenment is something for you to shoot for, it is a thing to be experienced and once it's experienced the heavens open and the sandalwood manifests and the multi-faceted jewels begin to rain down from the heavens! That can kind of give you the courage and the chutzpah and the vim to actually do the practices that, as we've repeated, one needs to do. As long as there is a doer there, as you have said, something needs to be done. But it can also lead to this trap of thinking that there is such a thing as a moment at which one is done once and for all. Instead, this notion of the endless enlargement is wonderful news!

G: Oh, absolutely.

R: I think many people take it to be negative news, because they think, "(*Sigh*) I'm never gonna be done with all of this stuff!" As opposed to when you really start to open, the fact that really what you've engaged on is this endless adventure filled with continual surprise, is the best of all possible news.

G: Absolutely, yes. Yes, as you come across obstacles too, on the path, it's, "I'm enlightened, I shouldn't be having this obstacle.

I must have done something wrong! I need to go back!"

R: "Yes, excuse me, um, obstacle, I don't think you quite understand who you're talking to here! The hat, the aura… uh, you are clearly intended for someone else!" It's well, "No, I'm here. I am a problem in your awareness." Sometimes if there's been progress, and then something "negative" happens, it must all be false, or "I must have done something wrong", "I must have sinned", and "Ohhhh, I had it and now it is gone! What am I going to do to get it? I've got to get it back!" That is opposed to saying "Ooohhh, welcome guest to the House of Being, welcome! What is it that regret has to teach me today? What is it that remorse has to teach me today? What is it that joy has to teach me today?" As long as there's somebody there to experience an obstacle, then the obstacle is a gift.

G: Well as we have seen, it seems as if the obstacles—either they become more apparent or they do get more difficult. If we have this anthropomorphized version of Universal Consciousness as something that's trying to awaken (and evolve) Itself (or Herself), then perhaps She just keeps doing more and more difficult challenges. It seems like the ante keeps going up and you keep getting deeper and deeper. The more difficult the obstacles are that you face and the more you come into them and be present with them, the deeper and more still the whole thing appears to get. There is this ongoing enrichment in which, even though it's still, you think it can't get any better, there's nothing you could possibly bring in that would improve it or take away that would improve it, but yet at the same time it does get deeper and more still and more quiet and sweeter. So the things keep coming up, they keep getting met, dealt with, and the thing does get deeper and deeper.

R: And more beautiful somehow.

G: Oh, yes, yes.

R: So this idea of the obstacle as a gift has been really useful in my experience.

G: Well, when people first start meditating and they say, "Oh this meditation is horrible, I have all these things that come up and (*eewwww*)!" They just weren't looking before— now they're looking. But further on down the road where you start getting clearer and clearer and clearer, you look around the pond and there are a few bumps here and there. It's important to remember that we have 100 trillion to 500 trillion synaptic interconnections. If only 10% of those have anything to do with what we're talking about, you're still looking at trillions... 10 trillion synaptic interconnections, or more. Thank god, they don't become unwired all at once. There is a...

R: Yes. (*Laughs*) When they do there's a problem.

G: There's a problem! It's a gradual process of going deeper and deeper. We believe that what's happening is that these neural networks that are blocked up, these old stories and old memories and fears and pains and desires, begin to unravel. As they do, then things improve and real estate's freed up. The brain seems to be parsimoniously inclined, so it goes around hunting for real estate that's not being used. If these haven't been used, there's a big rock there, the brain says, well do you care about this thing? So it cleans these things out over a long course of time. Things that you hadn't even thought of for maybe decades, pop up... and you say, "What did I possibly do to cause that thing to pop up?" You didn't do anything! There's nobody doing anything, the brain's running the whole process and the brain's just found some real estate that's not being used and it says, "How about this thing? Do you care about this thing?" Then you meet that, but don't take delivery on the package, and it goes away.

R: It feels, because the sweetness continues, like, as you put it, the ante is upped. So it's, "Okay, so we've dissolved all these places where you seem to have had attachment to x, y and z. Oh! Here's z prime! How are you going to deal with z prime?" You say, "But I already dealt with x, y and z!" But, if you say, "Oh, yes, actually, wow, I forgot all about z prime. I didn't even know z prime was an issue for me, I guess that's why x, y and z were in the way and... yes, let me see who sent z prime. To whom is it addressed? No thanks." (*Whoosh*)

It can feel like the ante is upped because there does seem to be something more almost primal and maybe even developmental about some of the things that were below our threshold of awareness before. I've had experiences where I realized that I was experiencing, not in a kind of re-enactment way, but that I was dealing with the trauma of breaking my legs when I was two and a half years old. I had no idea that that was even in there.

G: Still hanging around.

R: Yes. But it was the same kind of thing. It was "Oh, well... legs feel great!"

G: These things "I have attached to, having broken my legs..." is it still useful? They're not useful any more. They're stories from long ago, and what your grandma thought about your playing soccer or whatever.

R: Oh, let's not get into that! (*laughs*)

G: (*laughs*) It doesn't matter, it so doesn't matter. So this "let go, let go, let go"... could you let go of this thing? You're only hanging onto it because you think it has some kind of protective value. In fact it doesn't, it's something that's never going to happen again.

R: It didn't even happen to you! (*laughs*)

G: No, exactly!

R: Endless enlargement.

G: Endless enlargement.

Functioning without thoughts: sex, psychedelics and non-duality

G: If you're in this totally present, non-dual, state then in fact you're much more "here" than you normally are or than you would have been 'before'. Previously, you would have been thinking about how it was last time. What protocol do I use this time? What does she like, or what does he like? How do I go through this thing? You're not even there for the event. You're someplace else in your head... you're unavailable to the person. You can't be sensitive to what they're feeling right now, what's happening for them. You really take what could be a great experience, sexually, and you turn it into something that's mediocre. The more you do that the more mediocre it becomes. You can come to this thing, very fresh, open and empty. It becomes a different experience. But even at that, it still pales in comparison with what we're talking about with non-dual states.

R: Yes, part of the non-dual perspective and how it's different and better than sex, and different and better than the ecodelic experience, is that you can superimpose it, or it becomes superimposed, on all the different standard brain states that you have, all the different experiences. If you can carry that with you, you can be present during each of those...

G: Oh, absolutely.

Mark: You can be present with the emotions of grief, the elation of success and really relate to people in a different way.

G: Right, but they aren't simply additives. This whole

comparison study that we did on relative pleasure showed that psychedelics scored nine and a half, this non-dual state ten, and sex was about an eight. But they don't simply add up. If you are in the non-dual state then you do sex and drugs…

R: Seventeen and a half!

G: (*laughs*) You don't get twenty-four or something. It does make you, though, if you're in this non-dual state, present for whatever comes up. You are available and present for everything, even seeing the beautiful leaves that are turning. You can be fully present for that in a way that you aren't normally, and that can be a tremendously deep experience. You're present for everything that comes up.

R: That's sort of what feels psychedelic about it to me, is that I can just be riding my bicycle down a road and then I stop and I look at those corn stalks that are ready to be harvested and just blowing in the breeze a little bit making this sound (*cool sound effect*). It's beyond words! I could stand there and stare and experience that for eternity, and it feels like that when I'm doing it.

Mark: Yes, that's one of the things that I learned about psychedelics—and I'm sure other people have written about this—that if you just relax your eyes and your ears and your ego recedes, you'll start to see hallucinations. Hallucination is nothing other than less interpretation of the perception. If you just let your eyes go, all these little things are already there in your vision, you just look past them as you're filtering more when in standard consciousness.

R: Right, it's what Huxley called "the reducing valve" of ordinary consciousness as opposed to the mind-at-large. But what's interesting is then you can walk around and, you're right, you can accept, you can be in this kind of sensory, cognitive soft-eyes mode of just accepting all things. Then what happens is that you see beyond even the "hallucinations", and it's as if you're seeing the divine ground behind everything. It is obviously classically difficult to put into words, but there's a kind of glow to everything that starts to emanate. What you notice more and more, and it is almost like the objective aspect of that "being held" that you talked about in another video... The more you let go the more you just feel that the world is you and the world is holding you.

Mark: If it's the background radiation from the big bang, the three degrees of...

R: Hallelujah to it then! (*laughs*) Yes, exactly...

Mark: It's the unity of the universe...

R: Yes.

Mark: ... that you're relaxing into and accepting and seeing those connections... not seeing the separations.

R: The static aspect of "we are here now and everything is solid and static and nothing must change because I feel this", leads to the feeling that I must hold onto this perfect moment for ever, "Uh, where is she?" But instead, as you're saying, if you kind of relax into the fact that you're involved in this ongoing big bang, it's beautiful.

G: Well you just... you just go away. You just get out of the picture. Back to the Eckhart Tolle discussion with Oprah, he did say he could understand how LSD would help people because—and I'm a complete virgin on psychedelics, so I'm speaking completely second-hand—but he said "I could see this could help people because it does jam up the circuits and there's no space for anything to happen inside except to be present because everything else is jammed." I can see why he was saying what he was saying from what you're relating. It's just getting out of the way.

R: That the goal is as in the subtitle of these dialogues: *Beyond Thought*. This is another taboo which never even occurred to me, being somebody who lived so much in his head, that the goal was actually not better thoughts, not more intensely creative thoughts. Those are all beautiful things, but "no thought"? This was not on my radar—not even as a concept—so much so that when it … *happened*, when there was a total silence of thought, I walked around the next day saying "What is this feeling? It's unbelievable." I simply prayed to this feeling and gave thanks for it—I was enchanted with it. To put it in context, I was in Peru at the time and this was one of my most powerful ayahuasca experiences.

G: Yes, we've talked about this ayahuasquero who spoke at the Towards a Science of Consciousness Conference in Stockholm. He went through his plenary talk and then he said, "This is all about having no thoughts." Here is an ayahuasquero… Why is he saying the same thing that this whole process is about? It's all about having no thoughts. It led him to that possibility.

R: Right. I feel like that needs to be repeated over and over again in fact because of what some of my students say in classes. First they say "Selflessness is going to be totally boring." Yes so we got with that one. Then they say, "That's easy for you to say, professor!" Or, for a retiree, "But I have to get up in the morning and I have to work in this job and then I have to go to these classes where these people are all addressing me *to* think." What's beautiful is to remind people that in fact you're going to be able to do all that, and you're going to be able to do all of that better, with more alacrity, with more aplomb, with more insight than you're going to be able to do when that version of yourself is trying to think for the situation.

G: Right. Yes that was, as we talked before, my biggest surprise, because I was running a big operation, had a big job, and I believed I was thinking all the time and making things happen, and then... there were no thoughts there. I found myself to be much more effective afterwards than I was before! I can't imagine "going back". People ask, "Would you take the blue pill and go back?" I said no, I just can't imagine anything less appealing than going back.

R: (*laughs*) So no, you wouldn't go back.

G: No! I can't imagine anybody going back! One of the great things you taught me was, you said that on ayahuasca there was a period where you'd taken this stuff and it was going to last a certain time and it was going to be over. So you had no control, but you knew it was finite. You said the scary thing about non-dual states is that, "I may not come back." Now you say well, god, what if I had to go back? (*laughs*)

R: (*laughs*) Exactly. Well it's really true. An analogy that happened to me yesterday is I was with my wife, and I was holding her and she said, "Oh I hear your heart, I hear your heart." I said, "Oh, what does it sound like?" She said, "Ba-bum, ba-bum, ba-bum, ba-bum..." Then she started to get tired from saying it, so much that I was like, see? My heart just does it, but if we try to do it on purpose we get exhausted.

G: Oh, yes... not good, not good.

R: I think that there's something profound in that: just like, let your heart do it, and everything will come to you. You don't need to do it for your heart.

G: But there's no conditioning in our culture right now to support that way of doing it—or, rather not doing. The conditioning is all "You must do this thing and this thing and have this drug and take this pharmaceutical... you must do all these things." In fact you don't need to do anything. You just need to get out of the way. If you get out of the way, then amazingly, double-triple amazingly, everything takes care of itself "mo better" than before... much, much better.

R: How is my heart going to beat if I don't tell it what to do?

G: My heart will beat and I'll talk just like I always have talked, even better, and I'll do work, complicated work like we always did, only better. All that happens is that you just lose this self-referential "blah-blah" narrative. It's just quiet in there. I just can't imagine taking a blue pill.

R: No.

Getting to stillness in a crisis...

R: Of course this means, as we discussed before, everything is just as it is, and therefore perfect. That means that even the organizations that we find ourselves working in, despite all appearances (*laughs*), are perfection too. Or do you think otherwise?

G: Perfectly imperfect. (*laughs*)

R: (*laughs*) Exactly. I'm just wondering how we might talk about the migration from this practice of cultivating an awareness of Source by dwindling the thoughts—the self-referential thoughts that we get from narrative mind, which, to a lot of people at first sounds very kind of almost selfish. How do we then get from there to this problem of the larger collectives of which we are a part?

G: We evolved, in a Darwinian sense, to participate in large organizations. We're the most social animal on the planet. Nobody else does the kind of organizational stuff we do. We have a huge prefrontal cortex, frontal cortex, dedicated to social issues, how to function socially, so we live that way. The question is, "Okay, given that we're involved in structures of some kind, can we somehow bring a whole different way of operating into those structures?" So however you organize it, whether it's your baseball team or it's your political party, can you bring some real differential creativity and intelligence to that discussion? I think that only by getting into (and this is Peter Senge's work at MIT) "presence", you get into "don't know", you get to a place where you recognize that nobody has the answer. Contradistinction with what we normally see with this party or that party or this company or that company or this university or that university has the answer—we get into "Well, maybe we don't know the answer. Maybe we need to look at this and say how can we solve this problem from a space of not knowing?" Then we allow something organic to evolve out of it that's totally different from what we might have thought of originally from the perspective of our traditionally split-up, balkanized world.

R: Getting into that space of "not knowing" also involves a different relationship with our emotions. When some news event happens or something terrible occurs, then there's very little just being with how terrible the event is. Just letting yourself feel the nature of that event instead of immediately linking to the narrative mind which immediately says "Okay you know...

G: Do this!

R: ... what are we going to do about that? Or how could that happen? Or, just actually just being with it. Don't try to even explain it remotely. Even the question, "How could somebody do that?" Not helpful! The level of just being with what occurred—there's a feeling associated with that, that at first for people because they haven't felt it in a while, it feels very bad, it feels even a little bit sickening. But to me, back in my days of psychedelic exploration, that's the beginning of the feeling. There can be a very kind of difficult period at first that you have to ride through and let go of. If you can be with that feeling and really look at the kind of trauma and tragedy that sometimes occurs, but at first we recoil from that. In fact, the "I" recoils from that. But if we can know that on the other side of that is another feeling, a qualitatively distinct feeling from that kind of sickening anguished first feeling of 'My god what are we?' then you can really be with it and you can feel real compassion for what's going on and then you precisely don't know. You don't have an immediate "Okay make that so, make that so." It seems to me that what would come out the other end of that politically will be something much more interesting, even if just as perfect as we have now.

G: I have no experience with psychedelics so I can't speak to that. But I think you're onto a point about when you see something awful happen, whether it's "man-made", or "natural," horrific things. You immediately run off into "I must do something, I must..." You can feel the difference, the shift in your energy. As you said earlier, if you can just be present to the change in yourself—from however you were before to how you are as that event happens, then you can posit yourself back to "Okay why did I leave this space?" In this new space I've moved into, this, "This is horrific! I must do something! I must understand this thing!" We have lots of media feeding it now, too.

The media feeds it with throwing boxes and boxes of gasoline and tinder on the fire to get it burning faster and faster because that's how the media operates. If you can just pull yourself out of that, and you did a media fast for quite a while, which can be very, very salutary, and you pull back and say, "Okay, what if I weren't listening to the media? What if I just took the event, saw what I saw, and then let go? I didn't spend hours and hours and days and days and days whipping myself into a frenzy with this media-fed wildness that we get into." Just stay out of it.

R: Right. Imagine if people spent even a tenth of the time in Source, in Presence, in the space of no thought, in the space of not knowing—as they do in that kind of media feedback frenzy about "What are we going to do about this now?" The effects of that alone would be quite salutary. I found a media fast to be an absolutely fundamental part of my path because I was living in that space of constantly getting my chain yanked by people, who again are just marketing the idea that the world is broken. Each day features a different aspect of the way in which the world is broken, and that gives a kind of unending source for our attention that needs to be focused on that. That's how they make a living and that's fine. But on the other end, we are beings who are capable of directing our attention not towards the content of the narrative mind, "What are we going to do about this?", but just towards the way we are in any given moment.

In that sense these horrible traumatic events that occur all around the world periodically are reminders to us to stay in that present moment and really feel. Not only are we not feeling that when we have that immediate response, we're not feeling the emergence of the first violets in late April in Central Pennsylvania, we're not feeling the particular look on someone's face as you pass them on the street, we're not feeling the sound of a bird singing, we're not feeling, we're not being with any of it.

G: Perhaps a response might be inculcated that the next time I see a traumatic event on media being forecast and going crazy (now with social media we can really blow these things up very, very quickly) is that folk just give themselves a one-day media fast in the middle of the complete craziness when all you see on all the media is that one thing. Just give yourself one day of, "I'm not going to watch anything on the media" and see how you feel that day. See how different your space is, your consciousness is, because you're not being whipped into a frenzy. It will give you an idea of how much you can distance yourself from all of this craziness just by a simple act of saying, "I'm just going to turn it off for a day." Watch what happens. That will show you what you can do in Stillness.

R: Then you can even practice that, then you say, "Okay I'm going to do one day" and then you see how it works. Then you say, "I'm going to do three days" or "I'm going to do a week" or "I'm going to do two weeks" or "I'm going to do a month." What's really interesting about that then is the narrative mind says to us, "Well you need to know what's going on, you know that's totally irresponsible!" Yes, what's really interesting, and I don't really quite know how this can be, but you know absolutely everything that you need to know about what's going on. You're not insulated from it on an informational basis. What you're insulated from is the emotional affective frenzy of "for and against", "this or that", kind of constant chain yank again. You know everything you need to know, and then, from the space of being in Source, you can do whatever you like. You can turn the media on again, or not turn the media on again, it doesn't matter. But that initial chain yank has to be overcome.

G: That was a great lesson I learned... that was forced upon me. I was in nuclear submarines for five years and we were out underwater for three months at a time with no communications...

R: Wow.

G: ... for anything like this. So you found out that in fact everything you needed to know was just fine, and your world was very busy, very interesting. When you came back up they said, "Do you know that this happened and this happened and ... ?" You caught up right there. Bobby Kennedy was killed; I was underwater for that. I was underwater for Martin Luther King's assassination; didn't know anything about it. I missed the frenzy around those things. I still had the information when we got back, and it didn't matter to the world that I wasn't in touch with them for three months at a time. It was really a great lesson for me, my own media fast, imposed upon me.

R: Mine was imposed upon me too but by the cosmos, right? (*laughs*)

G: (*laughs*)

R: But no, it's brilliant because, the analogy that immediately comes to mind is of a soap opera, a daytime drama that you don't watch for three years and then you tune back in and maybe there's been some plastic surgery in the meantime…

G: Not much has changed!

R: Absolutely nothing has changed. Yes there's been some different person come out of a coma, or gone into a coma, but that sense can be very liberating. You can see that it didn't matter at all to Robert Kennedy or to Martin Luther King or their families that you didn't witness their murders at a distance.

G: Yeah, that's right.

Guessing others' minds through mirrors...

R: I'm wondering what you think about mirror neurons.

G: Not many animals have them and we humans have far and away more than other primates. Current thinking is that these neurons help us pick up on somebody else's position in the hierarchy, and their behavior. "Is that action really favorable to me or unfavorable?" "Is she going to throw me out of the tribe? She's the alpha female and I think I may not have done the best thing with her, maybe antagonized her in some way."

R: You're screwed.

G: Yes exactly! If you were thrown out of the tribe you were gone—you'd perish. The idea was to interpolate my experience into what I see in her behavior and try to mirror this back and understand in a way that I can guess what's going on in her mind. We don't ever really know. We just have this algorithm set running that these actions, those motions make me believe I know what she's thinking, when in fact I don't really know, but I can approximate.

R: They're "good enough for government work" as it were. They're good enough to be probabilistically favored in social life.

G: Yes, probabilistically favored. People believe they can read others' minds through this approach, and that works sometimes. But you must make sure you have the same algorithms running in your mind that they do in their mind.

R: I knew you were going to say that. (*laughs*)

G: (*laughs*)

R: At least I thought I did!

G: There's a presumption that all minds work alike, but we know all minds don't work alike. Some people may be running a completely different operating system, and so you can predict behavior of someone and be completely wrong. They asked Ramana Maharshi, how can you tell if somebody is awakened or not? He said (paraphrasing), "Well you can't tell." They said, "Well! Look at his actions, he acts this way and that way so he must be or must not be awakened." Ramana replied, "You can't tell."

You can't tell by that approach at all if someone is awakened. Actions are no predictor. What our mirror neurons will tell us from what actions are occurring, about what they must be thinking, just isn't accurate. Ramana's saying, and we find the same thing, that you can't do that, because the actions are no reflection of what's going on inside, if there's nothing going on inside.

R: What's so interesting about that, is the way you describe mirror neurons here, it describes why it is that we don't feel like our consciousness is our own. It encourages us to think that there is a kind of space of common consciousness and consciousness is outside of us, right? In fact it's very telling that Ramana Maharshi would say, "Well, you can't tell." Because, if you could tell, there would be something other than this experience of the pure field of awareness that we are, rather than feeling like there's this field of awareness here that knows that field of awareness over there.

G: Exactly. Right.

R: So part of the hump I find in just talking, working with people and teaching, and in dialogue, is getting to the point where we break the habit of simply understanding our own consciousness through the mirroring in another consciousness. It's not just that we're trying to guess at another's consciousness, but that that *loops*. Our own consciousness becomes, after a while, nothing but the guessing after the consciousness of another, never experiencing the capacity that is there underneath to be conscious at all. So that's very interesting because it explains how it is that consensus reality becomes so powerful in this kind of primate culture that we live in.

G: We are heavily, as you well know, lemmingly-like bred that way.

R: Oh, I agree with that.

G: (*laughs*) We evolutionarily, Darwinianly adapted so we could be together and cooperate, and the mirror neurons helped us cooperate. The ones that cooperated the best, survived the best. The ones that had the highest organizational structure and societal coherence were more successful. So we eventually have bred that into our species. Now when we see somebody who has a very different consciousness, a very different operating system, we still believe that they exactly think like we do, in "group mind". But it is not "group mind".

R: Then when there's evidence that they don't think like we do, we begin building a pyre... (*laughs*)

G: (*laughs*)

R: And we put them on there...

G: Then we burn them! (*laughs*)

R: Exactly! (*laughs*) It's very interesting because it says, "Okay, now we're in this point of the evolution of consciousness where we know about mirror neurons and we can be aware that that's a beautiful thing. We're here because we've been able to cooperate better than starlings and cheetahs and jaguars and bears."

G: Right…

R: But that doesn't mean that's who and what we are. We sometimes make this mistake through our mirroring. We understand ourselves entirely through reference to this external validation system, which, interestingly, is never really a validation because what's being mirrored is always second order!

G: Yes, exactly.

R: I am responding to the guessing of my guessing and their guessing and so on.

G: Exactly.

R: So if we can turn our consciousness around, and say, "Yes, okay, I appreciate my heuristic ability to guess at the role of the alpha male or the alpha female or any of the subdivisions of that that exist in our corporate world, but what about the condition of consciousness that allows me to do that?"… Then I spend time with primary pure consciousness. Then it's no problem that there's this thing called mirroring, but we don't fall for it in the same way. This really helps me because it helps explain how it is that I can hang out at a meeting, for example, and sit there and not do any of that anymore, not sitting there trying to guess how the other person's responding. I just am present, and in being present, inevitably there's a better outcome. Even though there's nobody there going, "Okay, and then when they say this I'm going to say that."

G: Right, right.

R: Because that is 2nd, 3rd, 4th, n^{th} order response to reality, whereas just being present is reality.

G: As you pointed out you could be in a meeting, and if you're completely empty, you're not participating yourself in this game of back-and-forth, back-and-forth, and the "I

Guilt and shame... useful or dysfunctional?

R: If you just let go, everything you've been doing all your life has been infinite rehearsal for whatever it is you're saying then, and it just comes out.

Mark: But what if you're ashamed, or feel guilty, and you want to edit yourself? Part of that is what society's given us. There are instincts for guilt too, I'm sure, the proper...

G: Sure, but that to me is what our "rider" ends up doing. The rider is the guilt carrier, the restrictor, the "holder-backer". If he's not there, as he wasn't in this case of Rich's recent presentation, where he just spoke spontaneously for 45 minutes, then it just flows freely. Only if you've got this holding back, this self-imposed curb, are you constrained from being freely open to let the thing dance. Let the elephant dance. There's this rider up there trying to hold things back. Let the elephant dance.

R: It's definitely the case that these episodes of guilt and shame are really important. You know that one of my professions is teaching writing to undergraduates, and this is the single greatest obstacle to them really learning how to write. Therefore what I've tried to gently integrate into the curriculum are ways of really letting go of that version of themselves which is very much getting in the way of everything they know.

We tend to think that guilt and shame are useful civilizing barriers to our unbridled primal selves and that without them we'll do absolutely horrible things. That may or may be true in some circumstances—although I really doubt it. They do turn out to be barriers to getting in touch with who we really are and doing the best possible work that we can do for each other. That same guilt and shame that prevents somebody from writing an effective paper on the marijuana legalization debate, prevents them from really seeing the merits of the arguments on the other side that they're attempting to address. There's a very practical way in which it's profoundly unethical, if you'll forgive some hyperbole, to be guilty.

G: I don't share the feeling that there's anything useful about guilt and shame.

R: I don't either but…

G: There's nothing that's functionalizing about guilt and shame.

R: I think I was just feeling guilty for not feeling guilty. (*laughs*)

G: (*laughs*) I should be feeling guilty but I'm not feeling guilty.

R: So, a bit of guilt!

G: I've not seen anybody that I've ever worked with who was benefited by having guilt or shame.

R: No, because it's always after the fact anyway.

G: That's right. I come from a guilting, shaming religion… that's what my religion did. That's how it functions. It's such a demoralizing… pushing people down, holding them back, and you see how hurtful it is for people. It just doesn't help anybody be anything. If you're really a bad person and you're going to do a bad behavior (whatever that might be) feeling guilty about it is not going to inhibit you.

R: No, it just makes you cleverer.

G: (*laughs*) Exactly, you just get more cunning about it, you're a much better liar. So I don't see any value behind those attributes at all.

R It's interesting that you're saying, "I come from a guilting, shaming religious background"; it brings to mind something we've already talked about. In the book of Genesis when Adam and Eve eat of the fruit from the tree of knowledge of good and evil, they become ashamed. It's not so much knowledge per se, rather the important point seems to be the eating of the fruit of the knowledge of good and evil. Knowledge of good and evil suggests a kind of subject-object split in the knowledge that there is the knower and there is that which is known. There is "that is good, and that is evil."

G: Duality enters the scene.

R: It's not so much that one falls into evil, it's that one falls into good and evil.

G: The duality. Yes, absolutely.

Mark: We've all made a misstep and hurt somebody's feelings or hurt somebody physically at some time, and that might be the one instance where that immediate sense of guilt, "I did something I shouldn't have or I acted in a way that was…"

G: I don't have any of that. I was from a guilty, shaming place, I was a driven deterministic individual who I believed had control of everything—and then my thoughts stopped. It turned out that I had nobody to be guilty, or successful or unsuccessful or be in control or plan… just nothing, there was nobody there. There was no logical place to go except, "There is nobody in control, there is no free will and it doesn't matter." Something else is driving the bus.

R: It was the idea that you thought you were driving the bus that actually led you to do the bad, whatever, things you had to be guilty about in the first place. In my own experience I would just make a slight adjustment, saying it's not so much guilt that does that as the compassion that one feels when one feels the suffering of other people, whether intentionally or unintentionally.

For example, this weekend I was talking to somebody and I saw that the way in which I was trying to help them actually was making them upset. That led me to adjust the way I was talking to them, but it didn't lead me to feel guilty because I was doing what I was doing. I knew that there was no bad place that it was coming from because there was no place that it was coming from at all. I was literally just beholding this person and responding to their query of how they could live with slightly less suffering.

I think that if I had had a guilty response, that would have puffed up my ego more as if I knew or ever could know exactly the right thing to say to that person outside of my simple interrelation with them. The way in which the guilt could then puff up my ego, like, "Well I know what to do with her because I made that mistake before and now I understand that the real way… " Well, no. Then, of course, it turned out in further discussion that she wasn't so much upset as she was moved. It's just that little part of me that was saying, "Oh you know, what are you doing wrong?"

G: Exactly, the ego came in, the "I" came in, began judging this thing, began feeling guilty about it, came up with the wrong response which is what the "I" does, and you went the wrong direction. You say "Well, this could have been all averted if we just didn't have the "I" come jumping in here with this, 'Oh her face, she's frowning, something bad's going on here!'"

R: Yes.

G: I don't see any value at all behind those behaviors. Those feelings, to me, generate an "I" which comes in as it did with you, and compromise your situation. It compromises your availability to be present for what's actually going on.

R: Agreed.

G: Because you drop some model on top of it.

R: We can return to something we said in another video which is that we can also see the evolutionary situation where feelings of guilt and shame would be selected for. Having an "I" would be selected for in order to demonstrate fitness over and above the way in which one was already demonstrating fitness through one's activities. If it was a PR man for your fitness, then guilt and shame would conform with Nietzche's ideas of what is needed to become part of the "herd mentality". The group bonding principles suggested that in some scenarios, "Okay, this allowed that group to live through whatever, as a group, even if it wasn't the most efficient way that they could have lived as a group." But those principles are no longer useful in the survival scenarios that we face now. Probably emptiness would have been a more useful survival scenario now, but evolution doesn't always take the most useful characteristic, only the one that works in that situation.

Mark: We went from an asocial species to a highly social species, so we needed that herd instinct and that ability to cast out certain people. That was required and you feel guilty because you think that if something, you're breaking the herd rules so you may deserve to be cast out or that may happen to you. But yes it doesn't really fit with moving beyond the social species to become an integrated species again.

G: To me, the guilt is a mentalized emotion of our fear. Our fear was being thrown out of the tribe. If we get thrown out of the group, we die. We get no more babies, no more genes, and we die. And so we were terrified.

Mark: So the guilt identifies the behaviors that we're afraid of.

G: Yes exactly. This behavior…

Mark: This behavior might get me thrown out.

G: Thrown out, I'll die.

Mark: Then often we want to switch that and make it anger instead. Because the fear is, we're going to be thrown out and we want to resist that, and a better response is, "Okay let me attack whatever it is that's making me feel guilty", or change the situation with some other stronger emotion.

G: Right. But as we've talked before, this is now counter-productive. It's so useless because almost all of our battles are mental battles with ourselves or with imaginary foes or problems.

Mark: Yes, we're no longer small groups battling against each other. We're not moving in that direction. It doesn't even matter… Yes, it's good to care for your kids, but if they're your adopted kids you will care for them just as much. There might be some minor instinct still toward abusing adopted kids more than biological kids…

G: Right…

R: Slightly.

Mark: Yes, but you know what we are so capable of, and really we're all like clones anyway. Our species is so similar from one person to the next that having this strong drive—whether it's competitiveness or a desire to really see your group suc-ceed—the loyalty thing should be, toward the species. I think Nietzsche was saying this too, right? You want to move and raise the whole species even more and not just the subgroups.

R: Not the institutions, not the nation states.

Mark: Right.

G: Some of your work is some of the best I've seen to disabuse people of this perception that I'm a whatever, this particular bunch of persons or this person. You see down his hall he's got pictures there of people's faces. When you lift them up, and Mark's[7] one of the best in the country of going through genetically "What is this person? What percentage of their genes are A, B and C? "Oh my, gosh, this person must be this kind."

I sent my grandkids' DNA off to be in this National Geographic-IBM type study, and they traced back to where the kids came from. We all came out of Africa, we know that, we all come out of Africa, and how they came out of Africa. It was great showing it to a seven year old who looked at it and said, "Oh, we all came from Africa." It's so disabusing to get the information out that in fact we did all come from the same place. We know roughly when we came out of there, what path we took, we know some people went West, some people went East over into India and China, we know that! Let's get over it, people! We're all the same thing, plus or minus not very much!

R: To loop back to the previous discussion about the unity therefore beyond all religions. What would we expect if we're all coming from the same planetary kind of origin? Of course, we're all essentially genetically, biochemically, physiologically,

---

7. "Mark" is Mark D. Shriver, who is an associate professor of genetics at the Pennsylvania State University in State College, Pennsylvania. He has produced and directed the *Happiness Beyond Thought* video. His research is focused on admixture mapping, signatures of natural selection, and phenotypic variability in common trait variation. A major goal of his work is to apply these methods and understanding of genomic variation to studies of common diseases such as type 2 diabetes, adaptation to altitude, hypertension, and prostate cancer. His research has also focused on normal variation such as skin pigmentation and response to UVR. More recently, his research has focused on the genetics of facial features. He has consulted for and appeared in several documentaries about ancestry, race, and recent human evolution. He has made public the discovery of his own recent West African ancestry.

like clones, even as we have particularities to each of us. Then we would be surprised if behind all these apparently different spiritual traditions they weren't exactly the same because behind all the apparently different phenotypes and temperaments that we have, we're all one.

G: Yes.

Higher functioning without thoughts

G: There is a tremendous resistance to "no thought". In my experience, I found that to be very threatening to almost everybody. They want to give, "Here are all the reasons that's impossible." I've gotten this from some of the top people in Tibetan Buddhism in the United States. "It's absolutely impossible, you can't do that, it's not possible to speak without thinking, you have to be thinking all the time… "

There's a tremendous institutional resistance because it's the same thing we're talking about with your examples; this is a real threat to many institutions: "If you people start getting happy, what's going to happen? What am I going to do?" This "no thought" thing scares the academics most of all. I know myself I was terrified. I really believed that if I stopped thinking I was going to literally die, just fall over dead. I was a compulsive thinker, and that's an academic.

So here it was—no thoughts, and I was still alive. That's been the biggest challenge taking this thing forward. Just telling people look, this is possible, you can do it and still function, it's not fatal. It's a big thing for many people to hang onto those, especially academics. We say, "Okay look you can parse this out. The part that goes "blah, blah, blah, blah" is one part of your mind. The part that does what you get paid to do—analysis, problem solving, and consolidating information—completely parsed out. One functions, the other one doesn't function. So you can keep your good stuff and lose your bad stuff." People see it as a big threat.

R: When people hear "no thought", they think "zombie". Whereas what you're saying is that there's consciousness which is going on "on its own", which has nothing much to do with the "I" thinking and "doing the doing". Then there is the aspect of our consciousness that has evolved in order to more or less take credit for and spectacularly display that, possibly for reasons of sexually selective fitness. The trouble is that it comes to believe that it's the whole story. As we let go of that particular function of consciousness which we identify with thought, thought as we would usually think of it actually goes on in the background, it's just that there's nobody there thinking it. Or does that not correspond with what your experience is?

G: Well for me, it's "still" almost all the time, and yet, functioning still takes place. We've used a metaphor which really came from cognitive neuroscience of the elephant and the rider. We have this enormous massive primary consciousness with massive computation capabilities and parallel processors and great storage capacity...

R: Designed by evolution.

G: Designed by evolution, which is all primary consciousness. That's almost all of our...

R: Do we have a percentage on that, like of what... ?

Let's just say it's an enormous percentage of...

G: Yes, but on top of that, as we've talked before, we formed this secondary consciousness seventy-thousand years ago, this rider on top of the elephant that does all of the self-referential "blah, blah, blah"—it was probably useful evolutionarily.

R: Certainly sexy.

G: Very sexy. But what we're trying to do now is recognize that this continuous talking up here, this PR guy that we carry up above here and say, "Well the President, or whoever, really meant to say this"—that person is quiet. There were some good research papers in the Journal of Cognitive Neuroscience in 2009 [8]on this, showing that we solve problems offline. We frame the problems up in the secondary consciousness, then they go offline, especially the complicated ones, the non-linear solution ones, they go offline. Sometime later the answer comes back up, gives it to the rider and the rider tells everybody else "I solved this problem." That functional state is unimpeded because it's all done offline; it's all done in primary consciousness. So all we're talking about is, you can keep primary consciousness, you have your graphical user interface—this talker to communicate to others and frame problems and send them down for processing. But it isn't there for all of the useless stuff, the stress-causing problems, the craving-generating, desire-generating functions just aren't there.

R: This is very consonant with my own consciousness even giving the talk that I just gave...

G: Yes! Yes! Yes!

R: ... at Psychedemia which was...

G: Beautiful, great talk, fantastic talk!

R: Thank you. I don't know who gave it, because...

G: You couldn't find him.

R: ... it's really very interesting. And that's what I mean by saying that thought happens in the sense that analysis happens, response happens, information is organized and responded to. Literally, my body was standing up there, I began, and then I don't know what happened. There was a moment when it was clear that I had some internal cue that it was time to

8. *Posterior Beta and Anterior Gamma Oscillations Predict Cognitive Insight*, Bhavin R. Sheth, Simone Sandkuhler, and Joydeep Bhattacharya. Journal of Cognitive Neuroscience, 21, 7, 2009.

wrap it up and the wrapping up came out of my mouth and I was done.

G: I've told you, without patronizing you, that was a masterful talk. And how long was the talk, was it 30 minutes, 40 minutes?

R: I don't know.

G: But a mass of highly complicated, interrelated information from many different areas, pulled out.

R: I had no… (*laughs*)

G: You had no idea how it was happening! But you were functioning at almost an astonishing level, just an astonishing—it was like, my goodness, this guy is brilliant! He's pulling it from twenty different directions in answer to all of the speeches before. This was, to me, a tremendous display of intellectual prowess and dexterity, and yet, you didn't do it.

R: No, exactly.

G: There was nobody in there. You couldn't have prementated that, because it was coming out so fast, so cleverly…

R: It's like playing the piano, you don't decide which fingers are going to go…

G: No, it was just coming out completely untouched. It was beautiful.

R: That's important to say because I think when people hear, "Oh well, Gary Weber stopped thinking", it's, "How does he decide what kind of a car to get?" Well, that's a different discussion, but it happens. In fact it happens with greater velocity and alacrity and depth than it does when there's this filter there saying, "Well, I don't know if I should say that, blah, blah, blah." That actually gets quite in the way and mostly what it says is, "Ummm."

G: "Uhhhh, uhhhh"... or, "It could be this or it could be that." You could not have given that talk if you had dropped down into that state.

R: If I'd been there. No.

G: You couldn't have given that talk. It was so on point, so fast... a perfect demonstration.

R: So that is what it means to be without thought.

G: That's how one who makes their living "thinking" can do it.

R: Right, exactly. We've conflated thinking with that reporter on the thinking...

G: Yes, Yes! The "blah, blah, blah" guy...

R: ... which is exactly the opposite because that reporter on the thinking is actually a very tight nozzle, and not much can get through it. Whereas if you just let go, everything you've been doing all your life has been infinite rehearsal for whatever it is you're saying then, and it just comes out.

G: Right.

How much should teachings cost?

R: Money.

G: Money. Show me the money. (*laughs*)

R: (*laughs*) It's not to vilify money, but we've experienced the way in which our common dialogue has been able to flourish in part because it is an exchange—but there's no exchange of money that takes place. At first I felt bad about that because I was starting to study Sanskrit with you, and I thought well this guy's just giving me this so I should be paying him for that. It does seem to, because we live in such a consumer and capitalist society that it takes on a different valence when we exchange money. What's the way around that?

G: It's surprising how quickly the discourse gets corrupted or changed... changed is a better word, as money starts to change hands. And I've been surprised myself at how little it takes to change the discussion. Even if it's five dollars it does make it very different, because it says, "Okay, if you're giving me five dollars to talk to me, then I'm obviously more impor-tant and more knowledgeable than you because I'm getting five dollars from you." It doesn't take very much to make it go that way. I do my stuff for free because I'm retired and able to do that, so it makes it difficult for some peers of mine, because some of them are just trying to get by, just trying to get enough money to survive where they're living. They say, "What should I do?" I say, "Go ahead and charge. You have to be able to feed yourself." We're not requiring you to not eat because that's the situation the universe has placed you in. You need the money to be where you are and to have some way to earn it. I'm all for that.

I haven't seen a donation model work very well for people. I used to be co-head of a local zendo here, and we used to do donations. One of the most popular things was the chanting that we did once a week. It was well-attended and it was exciting to folks. After a year we checked the donation box; it was zero. We got nothing. Not that we were going to get a lot of money, but we had a zendo and it costs money for electricity, heat, lights and all that stuff. Donations haven't worked very well for many people. I know some teachers on Facebook who talk about that and they were taking donations, and it worked. It certainly worked in India. India has much more of a culture of that, but in the US we don't do that much. Going around and just taking donations, you're liable to be very hungry. There're some exceptions, but most spiritual teachers that take donations are always really short on money.

R: Because there're the two sides to the problem, not only do we want there to be teachers but we want teachers to be able to make a living. The nature of the relationship changes for the person studying with the teacher, or in dialogue with a teacher. We could just loop around to Gandhi and say that, if somebody needs to make a living doing teaching, then they're probably also in a position to be renouncing the possessor, so they're just taking the money that they need to take in order to sustain themselves in a living. Nobody else is in a position to judge what that living is beside themselves, because as you put it, the universe puts them in a particular place and that's what they're working through. But it also, for good or ill, changes the nature of the person in dialogue or studying with the teacher.

On the one hand, as psychoanalysis has classically argued, if you make an investment, if you give money to the person, you're much more likely to incorporate the teachings, to follow up the teachings, to treat the teachings seriously. Because if this is a society in part that worships money, worships 'mammon', then you're voting with your feet as it were, you're voting with your wallet and saying, "This is something that is important to me, and I'm going to focus on that aspect of my life in a way that's commensurate with how much I spend on it." On the other hand, because we are a society that pays so much attention to economic value, I can imagine all kinds of scenarios where I am sitting here not in emptiness and waiting to see when we're going to get to solve the problem that I just want to get beyond, so that I can go and eat gourmet food at the restaurant.

What do you think some best practices might be given the nature of the existing system?

G: I'll take what was my experience. The argument that if I pay for something—which is the American way—the more I pay, the better it must be. If I pay two thousand dollars for something it's certainly much more valuable than something I paid ten dollars for.

R: Two hundred times more valuable.

G: Something that I paid nothing for is infinitely less valuable. That's a big motivation to me. I'll pay two thousand dollars and I'll learn a lot more. I haven't found that to be the case. I don't take money, but people I've seen pay two thousand dollars to get a lesson, don't learn much. They don't learn more because they have an expectation; they've made a transaction and they really expect a return on their investment, so the relationship really changes for me in a bad way. I've found by not charging, I've gotten some magnificent students—just wonderful people from all over the world. Some could have afforded it, some couldn't have afforded it, some had no money, and some have tons of money. But even if somebody has lots of money, you go to them and say, "I don't need your money, I don't have any interest in anything that you have." That changes it with even with the billionaires, literally, because they say "Oh, this guy doesn't have his hands out, he just wants to share." That relationship changes even though they have enormous resources. It makes the whole relationship so different for them from what they're used to. I have no problem coming across really exceptional people to work with. I'm very fortunate that way.

Even if you have to charge to stay alive, to feed yourself and your family or whoever and have a decent place to live in, you know yourself if you're pulling in more than you need, if you're really going beyond sustenance level and you're really offering your stuff without attachment. But it's so easy to get sucked in. As soon as the money starts to come in, and people start (*puffs chest up*), then the numbers go up, and the teaching starts to change. I've got some very good friends, who I've watched change their teaching as they've gotten better known and more money comes in. They change the structure and the objective of their teaching because it's become all about, "Okay, how do I get the most people? How do I fill the most seats? How do I get the highest values for their time being here?"

The teaching changes because you then end up not giving your teaching, but you give them what they will pay for. You start seeing your teaching change, and change and change to fit your market. It's a whole different dynamic.

Is your energy level important in awakening?

R: One thing that's easy to overlook in the wide array of practices that we're talking about here is physical practice, right? There's so much talk about the mind, there's so much talk about experiencing non-dual states where there is no opposition between the body-mind. I was wondering if you wanted to talk about the role of physical practice in your own experience.

G: Physical practice and recognizing you are a physiological mechanism... The most common mistake I see people making is what you just alluded to: the fact that we believe, "I can transcend this body and I can be completely beyond the reaches of this physical..." "blah, blah, blah"... It's not the case. This is a body-mind, and if you get extremely low energy, if you're exhausted, if you're tired, your blood sugar's low. I'm hypoglycemic so I'm especially sensitive to this. But it's amazing how many people get into huge trouble. Just like someone I was talking to last week, who was feeling very negative and despairing. I said, "You sound like you're just tired." She said, "Well I am exhausted." I said, "Get something to eat, sleep a little bit and then come back and see how you feel." She came back and said, "Oh that's fantastic, I feel great today!" (*laughs*)

R: (*laughs*)

G: It's just, it's like that. And she thought she was facing, facing into the Dark Night of the Soul and there was some deep dark horrible black void in front of her and she was exhausted and couldn't go... So well, take care of yourself. It really matters a great deal if your body is in decent condition, but you don't have to be fanatical about it. You do some exercise, get enough sleep, and get enough food... quality food. It matters!

R: This is right out of the *Bhagavad Gita*, if people need scriptural reference... and it's chapter 6, but I could be wrong. Krishna says, "Those who sleep too little... will not succeed in meditation".

G: Yes, exactly!

R: It's awfully simple, but, sleep! ... Eat well!

G: ... Grandma, Mom, whoever told you this thing, it does matter a great deal. If you come to your practice to sit down or to do an intense inquiry of any kind, it matters as it takes a lot of energy. The reason that we think it matters neuro-anatomically and neurophysiologically is that the default mode network has two key centers for selfing.[9] If you can shut those centers down then "blah, blah" stops. We've also found through the Yale work on experienced meditators that there are two other centers that are monitoring and control centers that watch to make sure these centers stay shut down as near as we can guess right now. It also shows up in the psilocybin work from the UK. Those two centers are important to monitor and keep the "blah, blah" network shut down. But these <u>are way out the</u> priority chain for the brain. If the blood sugar

9. The best resource for most folk for the next step in understanding this is the blogpost "Folk Who Meditate Decrease Mind Wandering" @www.happinessbeyondthought.blogspot.com/2011/11/folk-who-meditate-decrease-mind.html.

The relevant research paper is: *Meditation experience is associated with differences in default mode network activity and connectivity* by Judson A. Brewer, Patrick D. Worhunsky, Jeremy R. Gray, Yi-Yuan Tang, Jochen Weber, and Hedy Kober in Proceedings of the National Academy of Sciences, Dec 13, 2011.

starts to go lower and lower and lower, the brain's going to say, "Well hold it now, I can either do fight or flight, or I can maintain this watching thing over this default mode network which is a long ways away from my survival."

R: I'm going to do fight or flight.

G: Exactly! So fight or flight's what I'm going to do. So it cuts off the least important things in its view for survival, Darwinian survival, and goes back down its own food chain. The first thing to fall off, which is my guess, we haven't proven this yet, is those two monitoring and control centers. So if they fall out, the default mode network is back online and you start getting into "blah, blah". You can watch this happen as your energy level gets lower and lower. This is my blood sugar energy monitor. If I get narrative thought coming in, I know these centers aren't getting fed, and if they aren't getting fed then the whole default mode network control system breaks down.

R: This is very useful for practice, not only because it encourages us to have physical practice on a daily basis, whatever it is for us... we can find and feel our way towards what is appropriate for us. But also because when, as is inevitable, there is some moment of low energy, minor illness or pain or something that we can have awareness that, "Oh, I'm just tired" or "Oh, I'm still waking up" or "Oh, I need to eat something" or "Oh, I need to tend my foot"... instead of saying "Oh my god! This is it! I've really lost it. This has all been a sham!"

G: (laughs)

R: By definition as you laid it out neuroanatomically, there's no observer consciousness there that's able to get in and say, "Hey wait a minute, you're just tired", right?

G: Yes.

R: Unless we imprint that, install that in advance and say "Most of the time at a certain point in your practice, there are going to be bumps", right?

G: (*agrees*)

R: Most of the time, I would say 99.999%, those bumps for me these days are physiological in nature.

G: Absolutely.

R: The hallmark of them is that I don't see right away that they're physiological.

G: Exactly! Exactly, exactly! You're sucked into them saying, "What's going on?"

R: "What's wrong?! Something's wrong! Ohhh, the world is just wrong."

G: (*laughs*)

R: "Everything's broken!"

G: "My practice is for nothing!"

R: "Black hole sun!" (*laughs*)

G: "Dark Night of the Soul!" (*laughs*)

R: "I was fooling myself!" Instead of just, "Why don't you have a banana?"

G: (*laughs*)

R: Why don't you get on your bike?

G: Yes, exactly.

R: Why don't you drink some water? Why don't you just (*breathes deeply*) take a breath. Why don't you just realize that you're a little tired, you didn't get enough sleep last night? It's the wheel spinning, in my experience, the perception by you that, "What happened to the bliss? What happened to God?"

G: (*laugh*) "What did I do wrong? What did I do... "

R: Ahhhh! Wheel spin, wheel spin, wheel spin. In the meantime you're not tending to your physical practice and getting into a state or a space where you can really let go of the concern for the physical body.

G: That spiral has great ability to turn itself right into the ground.

R: Oh, yes.

G: Once you get away from being relatively conscious, and get more in the range of (*panting*), you can find yourself screwed right to the center of the earth.

R: Oh yes, literally.

G: You knock yourself down there and you have no energy to get back out until you just collapse.

R: I'm just going to drink, I'm just going to get a little whiskey, and that's going to give me the energy to get back up. Then it's like (*pretends to drink the whiskey*) "No, okay I'm almost there! Alright, (*pretends to grab another drink*)...

G: (*laughs*) ... or whatever.

R: Doohhhhh!! This is how you get in the repetitious behavior of drug and alcohol abuse because you feel like you need to do something to get back to that state. There's no way you're going to get back into that state through that kind of physiological abuse. You're only going to get back to that state through actually tending towards the evolutionary nature of your embodiment, and not having to be an Olympic athlete, not having to be a triathlete or some kind of one half of 1% of the physical population. Just tending your physical embodiment on a daily basis and being mindful about it. The good news is that as soon as you start doing that, it really does seem like with the rest of the practice doesn't feel like it plateaus.

G: Oh, no.

R: Keep feeling better, and better, and better, and then there's a feedback loop between experiencing non-dual states and the physical state being better, and so on.

G: Yes, absolutely.

R: So physical practice, whatever it is, was fundamental to my own awakening. I wasn't even available to there being any such thing as "pure consciousness" until I had swum laps for many years and been on the bicycle for many years and reconstructed myself out of the kind of total physical despair that I was in.

G: Yes. It's important that people also remember that this "pure consciousness" doesn't go away. It's still there. It's just a question of how occluded it gets to be. If you get into one of these "low energy death spirals", you find yourself completely occluded. Then, you can't possibly get enough stuff out of the way to be able to see that consciousness that is there all the time.

R: How can there be bliss there when I can barely breathe?

G: Storm clouds... exactly.

R: Yes.

G: Clouds everything.

Letting go into the bliss and joy of stillness

R: I wanted to return to this idea of letting go, which I'm always returning to because I'm always doing it throughout the day whenever I find some issue.

G: So, let go. (*laughs*)

R: Yes, and sometimes I even have to let go of letting go!

G: (*laughs*) Let go of letting go!

R: Exactly! One of the things that I think is important to explore in letting go is that it doesn't mean, in my experience anyway, just letting go of this or just letting go of that, although that can be part of your path. It is letting go of absolutely everything, and the kind of incredible joy that is there. I think that might be a way to start exploring the way in which surrender or acceptance or "thy will be done" are different languages for something which is an experience that is ineffable, actually. It qualifies as a mystical experience. When you really let go and experience that letting go—not just of this particular thing that's bugging you or that particular thing that you're worried about, but of *it*, of yourself, then it's a kind of oceanic feeling. It's just the liberation from this incredible weight of suffering that, speaking for myself again, I wasn't even aware that I was carrying around with me. It's almost a parasite on my consciousness that I have to let go of. What do you think about this idea of kind of amplifying the stakes of letting go?

116

G: Well, you're quite a ways along, I'm not patronizing you, but you're quite a ways along. So for you where you're experiencing what you're experiencing, that's a great place to be. The folks who are much earlier in their work seem to need something that gets them into contacting it. Byron Katie's work has been very useful, because it is a structured, very simple protocol. You just ask, "Is this thing I'm torturing myself with all day long, that goes on and on and on... is it true?" Just a very simple, "Is this thing true?" And folk say, "I never really thought about asking if it was true." So then you start looking, "Is it true?"

Even in the process of looking at "Is it true?", something starts to work. Then you ask, "Can you be certain it's true?" You start to look at it. Again, in just the very act of looking at "Can I be certain it's true?" you find "Well... not really..." Whatever the answer is for you, and then you ask, "How does it feel when you have this feeling?" If you've been torturing yourself, beating yourself, "blah, blah, blah" all day, you just say, "How do I feel right now? I feel crappy." Then you ask, "How would you feel if you didn't have this feeling...?" "A lot better." Then the fifth part after those four questions is to turn that 180 degrees. "Is this thing just as likely to be true if it changed 180 degrees?" Changing "Mary hates me" into "Mary doesn't hate me." Is that just as possible, likely to be true?

Those five steps, just used almost by rote, are a great approach—and each one of them has an element of surrender in it. When you say, "Is it true?", because you didn't question it, you've assumed it's true. Then you say, "Well, maybe it's not true." There's a release there, an "oh... " Each question gives you a chance to let go more and more.

It is learning how to feel what it feels like to let go of a belief you have, an unquestioned belief. It may be completely false, and holding that belief makes you feel very bad. Can you let go of it? Just let go of it. Those protocols, and the other

Sedona[10] approach of "Could I let go of this? Would I let go if it? When?" It appears that even if we consider it and say, "No, I want to keep this thing, it's fantastic, it's really useful, I love feeling this way, I'm not gonna let go of it, ever!", just the very act of considering it, whether it's the Sedona Method or Byron Katie's method, just considering this "blah, blah, blah" that goes on all day long, starts to weaken it. It takes the energy out of it and gives you a break, a respite to begin looking at it in some way that's prescribed and leads you down a good path.

R: Then, in my experience, you're on that path and you're doing that, and I'm thinking back to about a year ago, when I came to you one day and I had something that I'd come across that I couldn't let go of. It was basically my obligations to my job and therefore my obligations to my family. It was such a wonderful liberating experience to look at that.

I did it in almost that way, saying, "Well is that true, do I really need to have this job or that job in order to fulfill my obligations to my family? Do I really need to be anything at all other than what and who I am in order to fulfill my obligations to my family and to myself?" It wasn't like I just asked that one time and then it all fell away. Then I got proactive at it and started to imagine myself with other roles, like "Maybe I have a completely nowhere fast food job, and I'm dropping the fries in... and it's great! It's okay! Hey look, I'm talking to somebody next to me, and I'm sharing an experience, right?" So I was able to get closer to that state that Ramana Maharshi asked us to get to where we realize that we're not the events on the screen, we're the screen.

Actively imagining myself in other roles really helped

10. "The Sedona Method is a .... technique that shows you how to uncover your natural ability to let go of any painful or unwanted feeling in the moment. The Sedona Method consists of a series of questions you ask yourself that lead your awareness to what you are feeling in the moment and gently guide you into the experience of letting go." www.sedona.com

with the surrender. I found that I was getting in a kind of oscillatory system where I would say, "Well is it true? I know it isn't true, but what if it is true? Or if it is...?" I was still sort of trapped in that space of trying to figure out something in the past which was absolutely not available to me and likely didn't even happen.

G: Right, exactly. This may be not useful at the stage we're talking about, but if you can focus on "Is there anything that's not changing in all of this?"... There's this endless pendulum back-and-forth, and "She said, he said, I can't believe... blah, blah, blah"... If you can just drop back for half a second and say, "Is there something in all of this that's not changing?"... This may be difficult for some folk but just, "Is there a screen, a basis of consciousness within which all this stuff manifests?" Are we the movie or are we the screen? You can be either one—it seems like you can choose. I can be the movie or I can be the screen.

R: Pick your ground almost.

G: Pick your ground! Pick your ground and you'll live very differently in those situations. We're so addicted to being in the movie; running around in the movie, being a character and having all kinds of emotional problems, yada yada. There's another possibility. You may not want to entertain it. The other possibility is "What if you're the screen? What if you're just the space within which this all manifests?" The movie has nothing to do with you. The movie is just the movie.

R: Sometimes it's interesting, sometimes boring, but really you're just the screen.

G: You're just the screen. If you can consider what it is that doesn't change amongst all this changing stuff, you can get a big step back out of the story, out of the thing, and break that belief. You may have to go back time and time again, but if you can just keep looking for "Is there anything here that's not changing?"

R: It feels good to find that space that's not changing. Literally, there's nothing that feels better than being the screen. You can feel it in the pit of your stomach, in your diaphragm. It's just watching these things unfold. Some of them are beautiful, some of them are ugly, some of them are good, some of them are evil, but, I am.

G: The common experience is that we have this feeling of emptiness, a gnawing emptiness inside of ourselves that we have to fill it up somehow. Sex, drugs, rock'n'roll, whatever... we try to fill that emptiness, and it doesn't work.

R: Do it again!

G: Do it again, do it again, do it again. Do it hard! Find something else! Next level!

R: Combine them in new ways!

G: Right, but you find, in fact, that you can never fill up the hole. The only way I found to fill up the hole was to recognize that at some level you are the whole! (*laughs*)

R: I am the whole. (*laughs*)

G: W-H-O-L-E (*laughs*). You let go of all the stuff around it which is just the movie, and recognize that you are that space that you're trying to fill up. Don't try to fill it up to get rid of it. Recognize it, invite it in...

R: Be it.

G: Be it. Be that space that you're trying to fill up. Recognize that's what you are.

R: Yes, but what's so beautiful is that the reason it feels empty is because it's like a plant that you're not tending.

You're looking out at the world and tending the world, saying, "Oh, maybe try this one, maybe this car, this partner, this drug, this music." You say, "If you just turn around and instead of tending the condition of all of those things, you just notice that it's there, there is no hole, there's nothing missing there."

G: Exactly.

R: There's nothing missing at all. I used to feel that when I would go into a hotel room when I was traveling by myself, I would need to turn on the television immediately to fill (*whoooosh*) the whole room (*breathes relief*).

G: Ah, so I'm safe now!

R: Exactly. What kind of horrible thing will distract me from the fact that... (*laughs*) What I hadn't realized is why I was fleeing this Stillness, this silence, when the emptiness was being caused by me not tarrying with the Stillness and the silence.

G: We have this enormous fear; I had it too, of this Stillness. As you say, "Anything but the Stillness, anything but that!" You find out that it's really an incredibly sweet space. There's nothing dangerous or scary about it. It is unchanging, it's the hole we're trying to fill up. We do know at some deep level that in fact that is the truth, but we just don't have quite enough confidence yet. We're not yet secure that if we go into that space and don't turn on the TV, we can just be in that Stillness. It's just astonishing.

R: Even a hotel room seems like a beautiful, kind of glimmery place at times when you let the Stillness happen.

G: Absolutely.

R: I'm a classroom teacher and this is the biggest obstacle, I think, to good teaching. Teachers and students are uncomfortable with the silence that can emerge in discussion. Once upon a time, it would be like, "Argh, why aren't they prepared! Argh I'm going to have to come up with something to fill the void!" Now it's really beautiful. I have a morning class at 9:45 so they're a little bit... unfocused. I just sit there and when I ask a question and there's nothing, I can just have a little tea and I just sit there and really enjoy the silence. I think they're starting to enjoy it as well. When you do that, almost like a Quaker Meeting, something comes up, somebody does have something to say. But there's none of this obligatory filling of the void. There's no need even to fill that void by saying, "Oh yes, sometimes we should have silence too."

Then, instead of chasing what it is we need to get through in the class, we allow the class itself to emerge. That's just one more or less mundane example. Just becoming more comfortable with the silence even when you're sitting next to somebody on an airplane or bus or something... "blah, blah, blah"—then silence.

G: Ralph Waldo Emerson got together with an old friend whom he hadn't seen in a long time. They just sat next to the fire and were quiet for two hours. Then they got up and went home. They said it was the best night they had ever had. They had such rapport and such depth in themselves, they just let go into that space and being there, still, silent together was much more precious than just babbling on because you were afraid to not have something to fill up the space.

R: Even Michel Foucault, probably the most famous French thinker of the late twentieth century, writes about a very similar thing. Somebody came to visit him, they smoked some hash, and they sat there in silence for 3-5 hours, and it was profound. For somebody who is raised in the tradition most devoted to "parler, talk, talk, talk", to just let that silence come forth, and to really revel in it? Not some kind of "Oh it's sacred, shhhhh!", but just let it come out.

G: Ramana Maharshi taught mostly in silence. We have a lot of stuff written down about what he said to people when he did talk, but he spent much of his life in silence, certainly his adult life. It's really a very effective technique. It's amazing, in our culture, how just a little silence causes people to be uneasy; it doesn't take very much. If you get in front of a class and you don't say anything for a minute…

R: I would say… five seconds.

G: People get very uneasy. I gave a talk out in San Francisco and I just stood up and didn't say anything for two minutes, and it worked, and it worked. That's a different crowd though—thirties and forties and they're kind of into this thing. It really changes the dynamic in the room.

R: I always do it now.

G: You just don't say anything for two minutes and everybody pays attention, everybody stops talking, everybody's there, and the whole thing goes so much better from that space because you've created this openness, this welcoming… you say, "Look, it's okay if we don't say anything, people." You go on from there.

R: Robert Adams was a student of Ramana Maharshi's, then a handyman in Los Angeles, and then, begrudgingly apparently, started doing satsang near the end of his life. His recordings are available online for free. He often said, which I was really happy to hear because I felt this intuitively, that the words are just there to create the silences between the words.

G: Oh yes, that's like Miles Davis.

R: Exactly!

G: Miles Davis was all about the spaces. It had nothing to do with the notes. The notes were only there to show you where the silence was.

R: Yes.

Making awakening too complicated...
pitfalls and barriers

R: It's pretty simple, really. That's really what I want to talk about is this... the temptation to make all of this so extraordinarily complex. And when I say "all of this", I mean this attempt which we have to seemingly do over and over, to find out who we are and what we really are—which is pretty simple at the end of the day.

But, one of the reasons I enjoy doing these dialogues is to disabuse myself of the complexity that then comes up, right? Saying, "Ah well you know it's true that up to now it's proven the case that all I need to do is just get still, but now, now there's this new temptation/challenge/obstacle" and so forth. So, I was wondering what your own experience was about that, after the simplicity then the complexity.

G: Well, I mean for me it's very simple. There are a lot of discussions going on in different forums that I'm part of about what is enlightenment, what does awakening look like?, The 'e' word "enlightenment" should just be struck from the language. A simple definition would be, for me, we've touched on it before but, "Can you just sit by yourself in a room alone and be okay with what's there? Can you basically like what you see when you're just being still, alone, eyes-closed, quiet?"

If you don't like it, if you're running someplace else, if you want something else, there's something wrong with that, or you wish something else was happening, then you're not at ease. You're craving something else. If you don't have craving, attachment, you don't have suffering. That's easy to say and sometimes hard to get to, but you can easily look at that and judge it.

The whole thing gets simple but then the brain runs back out again as our brains are trained to do, because of all our education to run back out into complexity. We like complexity. We believe that's where we make our money… It isn't. Our insight really comes from getting information, ingesting it and then having it process offline, and then coming up with some insightful perspectives with more learning. But the ego runs there and says, "Hey look, I know this is not cool here, this quietness, this stillness thing is not okay. How about this complicated problem over here, this big issue I've got in my life?"

R: Oooh, labyrinth.

G: Or, I could be solving this problem, that problem, and then, stories begin. It gets simple and then complex because you keep getting dragged into it by the ego, the "I", or whatever words you want to use, running back into a place where it feels secure, back into confusion and disorder and complexity, when in fact the answer is really, really simple. The more time you watch that dance going back and forth, this arising and passing away as some of the scriptures describe it, the more you see that happening. You say, "Well I don't need to keep running out there, because it's so much better over here." Eventually the brain learns that. The brain says "Hey, this—what I have here—is so much cooler than that thing over there, so I'll just stay here if you don't mind," and it becomes more and more over here and it ends up residing in the still place.

R: Maybe that can be used for a heuristic then, in the sense that we can ask ourselves, "Does it need to be this complex?" When you go through some spiritual path and say, "Okay, now I'm going to this level, I'm going to get this initiation, going to study with this teacher or I'm going to try this practice." That's beautiful, that's opening a lot of doors, as I remember you telling me about, when I was looking at every single spiritual tradition on the planet. There is something beautiful about that. But what's beautiful about it, is the way in which they all converge on a simplicity.

When we start getting involved in making things more complex and finding special arcane angles that are going to be The Way (capital *T*, capital *W*) that we're really going to break through, then we might have a heuristic where we say, "Hmmm, is it really that complicated? How could it possibly be that complicated when it's our birthright, when it's what's already there, when it's what we're just getting in the way of?" So using this heuristic of saying "Is this complexity to be trusted?" might help counteract what I recognize as our love of complexity.

When I first had a big opening after my experiences with ayahuasca, one of the things that I had the biggest problem with was, *it can't possibly be this simple!* My mind was intellectualizing everything. It was convinced that the only truth that could be found was radically complicated, and you had to bring Hegel together with high-end topology, complexity theory, non-linear dynamics and the evolution of the quantum mind as it instantiates itself through nanotechnology. That's all fun, cool and interesting and it too has that simple core to it, but what I was doing was having my mind chase some complexity because it couldn't face the simplicity.

G: Yes, exactly, exactly. Yes, there's a lot of discussion going on about should you have levels or not. I'm not a fan of levels as you know. The idea that I've got a yellow belt, you've got a green belt and he's a black belt or whatever, that's very seductive. People love that. They want to be special. They want to be able to go to their parties and say, "Now I'm a blue belt or a first degree black belt…"

R: You should put that on your Facebook site…

G: It's on right now. If you look recently it's up there.

R: Oh, okay, alright, yes.

G: So you get this building up, and we're trained to do that. Evolutionarily we want to fit into a hierarchy, and this feeds that. We get dopamine and other neurotransmitters. We get all kinds of support for working our way up the hierarchy. The problem is, if you want to get simple, that you've built this massively complex, egoically-structured lattice. You get to the top of that and that's a big part, for many people, of their identity. So, if we say, we're going to get rid of this third degree black belt, we hear, "No! Don't take away the third degree black belt! That's who I am!". It is who they are.

R: Well, they're still badass whether or not they have that belt… (*laughs*)

G: (*laughs*) Yes, yes, but the point is that's their identity and you've taken the very thing you need to deconstruct in order to get simple, and made it really elegantly reinforced, and Darwinianly-supported. So you have this huge ego that now is trying to make the next step to transcendence, and they have to let go of the "I". That's very difficult. I work with a lot of those people and it's very difficult in that space. If you come up this ladder to try to make that transition over to "I want to go non-dual," it's very hard for them. So…

R: It brings to mind a kind of Yogi Berra-ism, in other words, that "You can't get there, you're too advanced." (*laughs*)

G: Yes! (*laughs*) I hadn't heard that one…

R: You've made too much progress, I'm sorry, you'll never be enlightened.

G: Yes, I love Yogi, I hadn't heard that one. It's a good one though. And I think that does happen.

R: Oh, I just made it up. It's not actually Yogi Berra—I was just channeling him.

G: But that's the whole idea. You're too advanced, and because you're too advanced you will never get simple. You've got to let go of all that structure that you've invested so much energy in, and so much of your ego is built around this, "Well, I really am a very advanced person."

R: What it brings to mind is some research that was done, I believe back in the twentieth century, that was reported in an amazing book by Ronald Siegel, called *The Fourth Drive*. It was one of the early books about the role of psychedelics in the evolution of human and animal consciousness... Interesting guy. He pointed to some research—and I think it was chimps, but it was primates for sure, and they gave them DMT. They smoked dimethyltryptamine, a very potent psychedelic, ecodelic. What they found was that wherever any of the chimps were in the hierarchy, they were affected differently by the DMT. If they were low down in the hierarchy they would freak out and evince all kinds of symptoms. But the higher up in the hierarchy they were in terms of what the primatologists called "alpha", the less they were affected by it.

If you meditate on that for a minute it becomes clear that if one reflects on psychedelic experiences—I know you're a perpetual virgin on that—but you realize that what it's testing for is, "Are you going to attach to something?" If you attach to something you're going to suffer. So what it points to is that if you really want to go n^{th} degree black belt and transcend, you have to let go of everything.

In a way, the psychedelics in this primate study context were a kind of measurement, a metric of how far have you let go of everything? To truly be alpha—we tend to think that alpha means like, "Grrrrrr!" you know, "I'm going to puff myself up and be on steroids and yada-yada-yada.", but in this context to really transcend hierarchy itself means letting go of any attachment whatsoever. This is again, to loop it back, pretty simple, and is the core of every spiritual tradition that I am aware of.

G: The whole thing of complete letting go is what makes the probability so low for fully transcending. People say, "Oh yes, I'll let go of my watermelon at Christmas." But you say, "Okay, will you let go of everything?" When you come right down to it, it's a very simple question, but it's very hard to do. That's what makes the probability so low on fully transcending. There's no special technique required. There's no special intelligence required. Anybody can do this if they're just willing to let go and persevere. That's all... Ramana Maharshi's stuff is very simple. But it just requires your willingness to let go of everything. If you do then it's pretty easy. But not many people want to go there.

R: Well it's interesting, because it brings up those levels that you were talking about. If you look at global spiritual traditions, and the perennial philosophy or whatever label you want to hang on them, humility is a fundamental attribute of any spiritual path. Even at first blush you can see that there's going to be a tension between practices of humility and third degree black belt. You know, like it's going to make it harder and harder and harder to be humble.

G: Right.

R: Right? I guess one way of looking at it is that you can get to third degree black belt and then take on the cosmos itself and be humbled—and, of course, everyone will be humbled as soon as they take on the cosmos itself. We have such a negative association, both with surrender, which is a synonym for letting go, but also for humility. We think of humility...

G: Negatively.

R: Yes… like someone's been beaten up too much and put inside their locker, and so they've been humiliated. But in fact humility is a beautiful, beautiful practice that allows you to see what's right in front of you.

G: Yes, yes. But you just keep letting go, letting go, letting go… Even at the very first level of Ramana Maharshi's practice of non-dual inquiry, it's very useful. Even if you don't want to surrender all the way or let go of everything, of all attachments, there's still enormous benefit along the way, as far as you are willing to go. It isn't nothing or everything, it's really more and more and more…. You feel better, as you know, all the way going along that path. You get lighter, you're less attached to things, you're not as heavily conflicted. But it really comes down to how much you can let go.

R: What's interesting is then our narrative mind, as we've discussed it, takes what seems to be pointers towards letting go and interprets them in terms of the body. As somebody who in the deep past had many suicidal thoughts, I can now see what those really were: they were pointers to total surrender. But instead of recognizing them as that, I said, "Oh, well, what it means is, go do this drastic thing to my body." That's because I was identifying with my body and identifying narratively with my body.

But in this context, this utter humility and sense of loss associated with suicidal thoughts can then be taken almost like a slingshot. We can use that energy saying, "Are these really pointing towards suicide? Or are they actually an allegory for losing your egoic self?" Because you can't lose your egoic self through suicide. In certain ways it's the ultimate act of egoic self.

G: Right, right.

R: But it's really just in this moment that I'm recognizing that that's what it was. I felt that I needed to surrender, and the only thing I understood about surrender was to surrender physically to the world. I'm just hoping that maybe if somebody hears this they'll say, "Oh, I recognize that!" And that what it really is, is surrender—not suicide.

G: Yes, the ego's in charge of the show at that level, and the ego believes it's not the problem. If you really ask, "Who has this problem? Who wants to do this act?" you can hold onto that question and say, "Well look, the body's not asking to be done away with." The ego's saying, "The body's the problem, it's not me!" The last thing the ego wants is to be deconstructed. If you can turn it around at that point, go back into the ego and say, "Well just who is it that's wanting to do this thing?" You can unravel that, unpack that somehow, to get a clearer look at it, and begin to realize what the real problem is here. The body's not the problem. The ego is the problem.

Nondual awakening: obstacles, tactics, misconceptions and delights

R: I thought what we would talk about is, of all things, war. You introduced me to taking a closer look at the *Bhagavad Gita*; I always thought it was such an incredible paradox that it was Gandhi's favorite and yet it opens on the battlefield and counsels war.

A lot of times when people find themselves on this path to "awakening beyond thought" there's an incredible sweetness, there's an incredible peace, and it's clear that that's all what we're gravitating towards. Oftentimes I find myself in that peace for long periods of time, and as I was mentioning before, it feels eternal. And then, shazam! Some aspect of myself that I have not yet worked through, almost by definition, engages in a massive sneak attack on the peace that surpasseth all understanding. And I'm in it, and I'm in something that feels very much like insanity.

So I think it's important to talk about that aspect of the path to awakening beyond thought which really gets you down in the foxhole sometimes. I hear people talking about sweetness and peace, and that is the destination, but there's also this aspect where what we're engaged in is a kind of a guerilla war with that aspect of ourselves which doesn't want to stop thinking. Does that match with your own path?

G: That's good. There're several misconceptions about awakening in general. One that we've talked about before, is that it is some kind of an Olympic gold medal, that you come to a point and you pass this thing, and suddenly, alakazam! You're done, it's over, completely finished. In fact, it goes on and goes on and goes on. One of the big misconceptions in the community is that there is a point like that. In fact, that isn't the case.

Even after you've had long periods of great stillness there's still stuff that keeps being uncovered. We talked one time before about how it's like you keep lowering the water in the lake. The lower and stiller the lake gets, the more quiet it gets, and you see things poking up that hadn't poked up before.

As a metaphor—as the brain is very parsimonious, it likes to conserve real estate and conserve energy. So what happens then, is it has found places that it's not using any more—big neural networks of clusters, sometimes emotionally-encoded, that are very powerfully, emotionally, locked together. As you've reported many times, when you go to those places and you do this surrender, "Let go, let go, let go", there is this great release, this good feeling, almost a rush that comes from this letting go of this very tightly encapsulated old memory or fear or old story. It feels like dopamine, feels like you're getting some kind of hit from that release, which is evolutionarily, Darwinianly, a good thing, because then it supports this cleaning out of this refuse or these conflicted parts of the old memories out of the 100 trillion synaptic interconnections, some of them not in the best possible condition anymore.

R: When you get that dopamine hit you say, "Ahhh, whew, yes, okay. Good job surrendering!" You let go for a while, and you're traveling along, life is but a dream, la-da-da. It's not quite like that but then there is this sense of increasing peace, increasing peace, increasing peace. It almost seems that as you go along in true Darwinian fashion, then the rocks that you hit are more and more jagged or sharp or somehow more primal and they throw you in a way that then requires different tactics maybe.

That's what I think brings me to this idea of war. It's not so much "Oh, I am in engaged in a war with myself" or that there's some subject-object relationship where I am fighting against something else, because, if so, then that war is going to continue forever. If there's somebody there fighting then you're going to have a problem.

Almost by definition when I hit these obstacles it's a kind of sneak eruption of that part of the "I" that is more or less holding on for dear life. It's learned how to either distract me from the tactics that have been working so far to even get me there, or that those tactics are somehow insufficient to deal with it. It's probably the former rather than the latter. It feels like war.

I think it's scary, and that's why I wanted to talk about it, because in my own experience I've often made certain amounts of progress—and then it's as if I'm totally lost and all of this has been just a sham, that I've just been fooling myself that I'm healing and that I'm getting better in some way. I just wanted to share that that's part of the process that you feel absolutely totally insanely lost and that's when you surrender. If you can surrender when you're totally and utterly lost, then once again you get that incredible release, and it's almost like the best joke in the world. What was I doing falling for that one?

G: Right. The standard experience for almost anybody when they start meditation is that they say, "OMG, this meditation's uncovered all kinds of bad stuff. I didn't have this bad stuff before. Now I'm meditating and it's terrible! Meditation caused this bad stuff to happen!" In fact all you're doing is beginning to look at it. Instead of looking out here, you're looking back inside, and you may find that it's a mess there. So you blame it on the meditation when in fact it's just that you weren't looking before. As you were saying, as you've gotten more and more still, you can actually feel the Stillness get more locked down, just feels it's getting deeper, and more stable... deeper, deeper, and deeper. Then something will come up.

R: It only has to be a ripple to feel like a mountain.

G: Oh exactly! Because it is, it's good in some ways and difficult in others. The good way is that because the platform gets
to be so still and stable, it's a better place to see things from
and to watch them. The downside is what you're saying, that,
"Oh my god it's been so still, now this huge monster rock has
come up!"

R: (*laughs*) … and it's a pebble!

G: (*laughs*) Whatever, it feels like a rock, it's like a boulder!

R: A stone, yes.

G: Yes, because it's been so still, now this boulder's sitting
there. As you say, your approaches need to change. People say,
"Well can I just take this "Who am I?" and use that question
forever?" I say, "Well, no." Because the ego is cunning. It's a
very slippery and sly thing and it will eventually find how to
blunt and defeat this incursion (to go back to your war metaphor). So you need to come up with other vehicles. Which
is why we do a lot work with 'where am I?', or 'I am not this
body' or do some chants like *Nirvana Shatakam* to try to give
other ways around the defenses that the "I" has just come up
with. You have to keep tricking the "I", coming around in
behind it some way it hasn't defended yet, find an opening
there which you can plunge through and make real progress.
But if you just keep pounding the same way, the "I" will find a
way to stop that. So you need different approaches.

Ultimately it comes down to what you say, that if you get
into one of these fogs where you feel like "Oh, my gosh I'm
lost, all my practice has been for naught! I'm really back worse
than I ever was!" you just feel back into who it is that's going
in there, and ask those questions: "Is it true? Is it absolutely
the case?" Then just surrender, just let go. Ask, "How do I feel

when I have this feeling?" Not good. So can I just let go?

R: What's so amazing, when I've done that, when I've recovered at some point and realized the need to turn around and look at who's having the experience—when I've surrendered—is that another tactic emerges, without any other input from me. I don't need to come up with the tactic. So, for example, what happened was that that strategy of just turning around didn't seem to have kept me away from the rocks; then I started to feel that I was just a drop of water within the ocean. I just call into myself a kind of ocean of nectar: instead of saying, "Okay, who's having this?" I just feel "ocean of nectar" and in that moment I don't have to do anything, I just am that Oneness, which is strength itself. So the war becomes—"Oh right, okay. So this was just a war *movie*, and I am the screen upon which the war movie is being screened. I'm not in this war. This is somebody else's war."

G: Right. There's been this something ineffable that's running this show. This gets anthropomorphic but we talk about Her as "Her," as a "She" who does this thing. There is this grace because you could just as easily go into this space of fog and stay there forever. You could never come back out of it again. Yet somehow, something happens and you find yourself back in your good place again. As you say, the right protocol somehow manifests; something you never thought of before, a whole new way and the door opens... another key goes into the lock, another door opens, and you go through that door.

To me this, call it whatever you want to, this recognition that as you surrender more deeply, and there's a good Gita verse about this too—you're *held*, you're absolutely held. We've talked about the fact that, for me, it was, you let go a little bit and you're held a little bit. You let go more, you're held more. You let go a lot, you find out you're completely held. Something, however you want to anthropomorphize it, something takes over. She's been there all along—but takes over and she keeps giving you new challenges. The challenges get more difficult—"Oh I've seen this particular class of problem, I've completely solved it."

R: Done it.

G: Yes, and She'll come up with something, "Well, okay... maybe not so much." She'll give you something that's just more difficult.

R: Right.

G: It seems to me that's the game. It keeps getting more and more sophisticated; as you get more problems solved She gives you harder and harder problems, like graduate school. But at the same time, if you push into it, work with it, She'll always come up with grace and a solution. So after a certain point in the process you don't have to do anything about it. Just be present, be open, go towards things, try to let go of them, surrender, and you find out that grace happens. Grace does come in.

R: Yes, it's beautiful, because when you're describing that process it might help remind all of us that this place beyond thought is anything but uninteresting. It sounds like "Oh, it's going to be totally dull. Selflessness is a drag. I won't want anything." But the exact opposite is the case because the intensity of experience actually ratchets up tremendously because of those iterating challenges that are being raised, raised, raised, raised as you go along. That's the adventure itself—it's a cosmic adventure. I think that I'm just at the point where I keep forgetting that there's going to be more. (*laughs*)

G: (*laughs*) That is a huge misconception, and one that I run into all of the time working with folk. Just this last weekend, they were saying, "Oh, this is going to happen. You'll just become a robot and this darkness is horrible, dry ..." I say, "No, it isn't like that at all! It isn't even close to that. If it were that, we wouldn't be doing it, we'd be doing something else. We're not foolish. But it is better than anything else we can find as we've done our study. There's really nothing else that's better than that." If it weren't that way, we wouldn't be meditating; we would be doing anything except that.

R: The grace aspect means that not only is there nothing better than this, but it gets better and better and better. That even just a day or so after one of those big bubbles of insanity that I went through, I can say, "Wow, thanks for that!" Because the other side of it...

G: Is even better.

R: Oh wowwww... I mean...

G: As far as you'd go before, now it's even further.

R: Yes, it's worth it!..., If there's anybody there to make the calculation.

G: Yes, yes. We've talked about the intensities of kinds of pleasure as far as you can subjectively describe them. We did a survey of some folks and it turns out that it's actually more pleasurable, this non-dual state, than entheogenics, as we call them now, psychedelics...

R: I prefer ecodelics.

G: Ecodelics, entheogens, whatever word you want to use, but more pleasurable than that, and more pleasurable than sex. If that wasn't the case, as the Buddha allegedly said, we wouldn't have any meditators. If sex were better than anything else, that's all we would do. Our culture gives us all kinds of messages about how wonderful sex is and yes it's wonderful. But in fact, there are things that are better than sex. If there wasn't then we wouldn't be doing them.

R: *Gasp!* (*laughs*)

G: (*laughs*) Yes, we wouldn't be doing them. But yet we find ourselves doing these other things, so yes it is very pleasurable. It gets more and more so. It gets so sweet you can't imagine not having it.

Oneness... What is it? How does it arise? What does it mean?

R: I've always been puzzled by this: that I spent the first 43to 44 years of my life just taking for granted not only that it was the external world that is real, and the internal world was just this kind of bewildering place where I never knew what was going on, even my own experience. I took it as a fundamentally given that the world is made of multiple *things*. It no doubt comes from childhood development, when we begin to discern the difference between things for very good practical reasons. But, as a part of this process of awakening beyond thought, one of the most crucial aspects of it, in the path, was realizing that no matter where I look, everything that I look at, everything that I encounter, it's actually all one thing. That there's no division that's really plausible that can be made between things.

And you say, "Well, Gary's over there and you're over here." Yes, but umm... Let's track the gas particles of our carbon dioxide that we're breathing out and the oxygen that we're breathing in. Or let's use some imaging techniques to look at the infrared spectrum where we are, and let's look at some other imaging techniques to see the micro-organisms that are in our environment... The perceived distinctions between us are, of course, just that. On one scale of course they're real; of course you're going to go home and I'm going to go home and we're going to carry out the aspects of the universe's work in our own ways. But this felt like it was a very important part of my path where I just kind of smacked myself in the middle of the forehead and said, "Oh, well I couldn't be separate if I wanted to be."

G: Yes, we can take many different approaches to that philosophically. To start with there's the fact that we're so massively interrelated, in the course of our entire day, that nobody can stand alone. You cannot step outside of the stream of events in your life, we're so interconnected. So from that standpoint, we're not separable.

When the page turned and the big shift happened for me, I saw it. I looked out and I saw it. "Oh, this is what they're talking about. It is all one thing!" It really is all one thing. You can see it's all one energy. It's all there because of your perceiving it. You can recognize the discreteness, as you mentioned, discreteness of objects. You can see the fact that they have different frequencies and different impact on your sensors. But in fact, it never leaves, this knowing, this deep knowing that in fact it's all one thing.

From a philosophical perspective you can ask, "Is it real or not real? Which is real?" The point is, it constantly changes, which by many definitions makes it unreal... it's changing so it must not be real in that sense. But there's *something* clearly that stands apart from this, that is unchanging and yet it is all one thing. It's a direct experience that there's no way to talk about other than that, as much as we've tried to, over the centuries, but you can't miss it. It doesn't leave, even when you get pulled into what looks like believing that it is different. Still, you can feel underneath it... "It's not real, this is all one thing."

R: I had read the philosophical tradition of this Oneness and been quizzed on it and so forth and was never persuaded by it in the slightest, because I looked out on the world and I saw multiplicity. I saw distinctions between things. And I said, "What are these people talking about?" But when it came to the experiential side, that's when I finally had moments where I experienced the fact that everything *is* one thing.

At first I found it almost frightening because it would sort of manifest in instances of synchronicity that had no business being connected to each other. But as I just kept going and kept releasing the fear that I would experience, it became the most obvious thing in the world. Titus Burckhardt, that great exponent of Sufism and the "perennial wisdom", wrote, "The unity of the world is the most obvious and obscure fact." It's obvious once you're willing to look at it. It's obscure whenever we're busy dividing up the world into good and bad, I like this, I don't like that, I prefer that over this, that one's good, that one isn't.

G: Cognitive neuroscience totally supports this. There's a great Harvard paper in a 2010 edition of the neuroscience journal *Neuron* which found that we have eleven centers in our brain that create this sense of there being something different from us and a sense of us being in time. These eleven centers function as a core of two centers and two connected sub-networks of five and four centers.

If one of the sub-networks isn't functioning, isn't active, then there is "no something else"; there's just the perception of there being no "other". The same thing happens with you in time. You live in now, now, now, because the sub-network that creates our sense of, "you past, you future, you present,"… that's quiet.

If you do non-dual meditation, or take psychedelics, what you'll do is you'll shut down the core of the network, which also shuts down both of the sub-networks, so you get the two classical mystical experiences of living in "now, now, now" and "All is One". You're seeing the true reality.

R: So in other words, the "separation" motif and the "past-present-future" motif that we experience in ordinary reality is a special effect created by our minds that may have had some functional value in different evolutionary situations, right? That tiger's over there, I am over here, I will make calculations. Or, the tiger was there before and acted this way and I know how to act now. But it's just that, though. It's a special effect that is useful for some situations and is not an attribute of reality.

G: The brain evolved that construct Darwinianly for some past time, and the question is, is it useful now? You can see that the truth of it, is that everything is all one thing, if you get that brain circuit out of the way. We only exist "now", which is Eckhart Tolle, only exist *now*. That's the other side of the circuit, us in time. They're just sides of this function-alizing circuit.

R: It's becoming an increasingly inescapable 'fact' that we're all one planet. And people are starting to notice that even beyond just the conceptual understanding, "Well of course I can come up with the money and I want to squander the fossil fuels—I can go from here to Korea," for example. I was at a friend's fiftieth birthday party the other night about thirty miles into Central Pennsylvania at a firehouse in the middle of a beautiful, very rural area. It is in many ways very timeless, probably hasn't changed much there in the past fifty years. There was a DJ for this party, and he's playing different songs and all of a sudden this song came on that was K-Pop, Korean Pop...

G: Oh no.

R: In this firehouse, in Central Pennsylvania, in 2012, where nothing has changed, and they're listening to this song which happens to have gone viral globally from Korea because you can get it over YouTube. The "oneness" principle is nothing other than what the computer scientist Ted Nelson called "intertwingularity". He was one of the early pioneers, archi-tects of the idea of an internet, and he pointed out that we were going to become increasingly spatially interconnected. Now the correlative of that is not just that we're intercon-nected, it is that we were never separated in the first place.

G: That's right. But it's so evident now. We can log on in milliseconds, or seconds certainly, and you can be connected to anybody on the planet. I Skyped last week with Singapore, Hong Kong, Germany…

R: I was in Milan this morning.

G: You were in Milan this morning, exactly! We are so interconnected. You can't step outside of this. So it's not surprising that we are recognizing that we all are one thing, now that we are so connected by our technology.

R: We should start to take that, interpret that, instead of saying, "Oh, this is globalization… that different powers are marching around the planet making the planet into one thing." What we're bringing out is the fact that the planet has always been one thing. Ten or fifteen years ago, if you wanted to make an argument that technologies alter human culture it was very controversial. People were saying, "Oh come on! It's just a tool! Human beings decide how to use the tool, and then that is just up to them."

But then ten years later and you're not going to be able to find anybody who will argue with you to say "Well, the internet hasn't changed human culture." Of course, it's a massive transformation. We're going to experience that… this is part of that experience of the transformation of human culture through the internet. There are feedback loops between technologies and human culture. You can't argue about it anymore.

It seems to me we'll get to that point about Oneness in about five years. Saying, "Well yes, I know we used to argue that it was a worthwhile thing to divide up the planet into these different domains because that was the meaningful distinction to make. It's just not a meaningful distinction to make because it's part of a special effect we've produced in our brains—it's not real."

G: Yes, it's a cliché, about how powerful the internet has been at breaking down the power of institutions. Whether it's religions or countries or companies, the information is so ubiquitous, so freely open and distributed in most countries that you can quickly know faster than your leaders know what's going on and be more effective at working in that situation. The first thing leaders want to do is "shut down the internet, shut down Twitter, shut down Facebook," because they can see the enormous power that gives to the people and what a threat it is to the institutions.

R: Institutions that make their living activating those parts of our brains which find distinctions between each other and relegating our thoughts to past, present and future.

G: Right. Institutions.

Mark: I think too, the idea of the physical reality of empathy that's been discovered through mirror neurons, going back to neurobiology and those discoveries... To me that's extremely fascinating and very powerful. I've known for ages we're all atoms and through that physical connection that we actually belong to the same substance and we share substance. But that fact that we do experience what others experience physically in our minds...

R: We can't not experience what others experience.

Mark: Right. So this empathy added to the communication potential now that we're all interconnected, is really expanding the effects.

G: Well, and this idea of awakening beyond your own personal identity, brings you into the sense of oneness. Out of oneness comes something that I call real empathy, where I don't do a bad thing to you because you're me, and I know that. They say that if you lose this "blah blah" person you'll become a bad person. No! You become a good person because there's no reason to hurt anybody because everybody's you. So why would you behave any other way? It's the golden rule—almost every religion has something like that. But you get out of being who you are, and then you'll find a totally different energy arises. You're much more empathic because you're not with an agenda in there. Stuff just happens as it should, appropriately and very intelligently manifesting.

R: There's a trick and problem of language in there, because sometimes people might hear that and they say, "Oh, I'm treating Mark with compassion because Mark is me," sounds like this narcissistic inflation of who I am. But if you just tried it you would see that it isn't that...

G: Everything's me. The cat's me, everything is me. So it isn't a question of "just Mark", it's everything!

R: Although Mark's special.

G: He is. Mark is special. (*laughs*) Everything is all one thing, and so it's *all* one thing. How can you behave with any arrogance because you're not anything either, you can't find yourself? You look and you say, "There's nothing in here that's me."

R: So it's not "Do unto others as you would have them do unto you," but "Do unto others *because* you are doing unto you."

G: Exactly! Yes... that's a great rephrasing of that. Absolutely, yes, that's a great way to look at that.

Mark: It really challenges a lot of behavioral science and science game theory—kin selection, group selection... these things were debated... Altruism—what does altruism mean if we really are physically connected with each other?

G: Exactly.

Mark: How do you do something that's selfish in that instance, if when you cause pain to her, you feel that too? We can come to ignore that, and this is a sociopath and how they would act in this situation.

R: You're right that it's poorly mapped by the idea of altruism because altruism assumes that there is a "self" there, who is then making some sort of sacrifice, according to one interpretation, or seeking some form of alternate gain, in terms of another interpretation. But either way, the basic principle is that there's no "self" there in the first place, and that the experience of there being a distinct "self" is the thing that is to be overcome. We don't need to increase altruism; we need to decrease the sense of a distinction between ourselves. If we do that, the goal of altruism is achieved.

G: Yes because if you look at a lot of... I'm not picking on my philanthropist friends but... philanthropy. If you look at philanthropy very carefully, even in your own actions when you think you're being philanthropic, you're doing it so that you feel good. You aren't so much concerned about "them". Watch very carefully. It's really, "I'm going to feel good about this because I give this poor, poor person this thing." In fact, it's all about you. It really is your own feeling. That to me is not altruistic, that's really very self-serving. If you get out of the way, a whole other quality of giving manifests that's very different.

R: And again, to return to the bible, the New Testament...

G: You're getting very biblical.

R: I'm sorry.

G: No, don't be sorry! (*laughs*)

R: I should grow my beard out. (*laughs*) Something about the bible makes you say you're sorry. (*laughs*)

G: (*laughs*)

R: 1 Corinthians 13, is Paul, and he says, "If I have the tongue of men and angels, and I have not charity, then I am nothing." But then he's very careful, and further down he says, "If I have charity and it puffeth me up" then basically it's not charity. So it's only this idea that if there's no "self" there in the first place, then there really is no charity. I believe that the translation is of the term *agape*, so there's no "self" there..." In any event, it's a love that is there, there's a pure giving where there's nobody there to give.

G: Right.

Psychedelics, sex and/or non-dual awakening?

R: What about tantric sex?

Mark: On mushrooms.

R: Tantric sex.

Mark: Combine all three together.

G: Well, that doesn't add up though. I put up a blog post about Eckhart Tolle talking to Oprah, and Eckhart, who we'll give him a mark for "Yes he probably is awakened", said he took some acid. He says to Oprah, "This is totally off the record right? "Oh yes it's off the record" Oprah said. He said that it was actually worse than his usual state, and it felt jangly and buzzy, and it wasn't as good, and it had some really bad side effects. That was Eckhart's first and only time, so you don't know. But Eckhart came up with the same conclusion that in fact this (nondual state) was better than LSD.

R: He recognized the state.

G: Yes.

R: He said yes, this is the state but there is a kind of violence to it. It's true, it was only his first time and he hadn't really learned to navigate the space, but I do think that, at least in my own experience, that that's the case. One of the things I'm grateful to psychedelics/ecodelics/entheogens for is that they served as pointers that this state exists. But, once you can learn how to occupy the non-dual state, inhabit the state, abide in the state without there being anybody there to take the psychedelic, then it really, in my experience, does feel better than that psychedelic/other state.

I agree with you, you can start to ration it out by saying, "Oh well, what about tantric sex on acid with imaginary infinite consorts and so forth." It's like, getting better and better chocolate—it's still chocolate, you know. It's still what it is, and yes it's preferable to other states that you would engage in in ordinary life. But I do think there's something so liberated, probably because there's less of me there to experience the everyday non-dual state, than there is of me there even in a full-blown ayahuasca experience for various reasons.

Again I'm only speaking about my own experience, that it does feel better and better and better, and it has a lot in common with the kind of cosmic adventure of psychedelics. I think the real taboo that Gary is pointing to here is that, as a society we don't even know, basically, that there's anything better than sex and drugs. Or sex with drugs. In fact, I can say that, at least for me, there is.

The thing to not forget is that you can also combine the non-dual state effortlessly with sex. We've talked a little bit about how there may be some sort of downside to that, that what happens is then it seems like, for some people, if they're not celibate then the non-dual state kind of decreases for a while. But I don't think we really have a big enough sample size to know if that's the case or if that has other variables.

G: That's a transient phenomenon. Say the non-dual state's here (*puts hand at shoulder height*) and you have sex, then what seems to happen, what feels like it happens, is that you still keep the thoughtless place. What you lose—some of the sweetness comes out of it. So it does—as we talked about— drop down some (*drops hand down to chest*) but it recovers very quickly (*lifts hand back to shoulder height*), even for an old person, it recovers very quickly.

R: We don't know any of those, do we?

G: We don't know anybody like that. But in a day or two, it's back up to where it was before. So this is not permanent. I don't know what it's like for twenty-five year olds, but I know there is that taking off. There has been this prohibition for as long as we've had religions and spiritual people around, to be celibate, which I think is really a big mistake. It generates all kinds of bad things.

R: Misconceptions.

G: We see misconceptions and it is not necessary, it doesn't help you. Nisargadatta, in his book *I Am That* talked about this, about *bhoga*, which is really to go into and experience it. Sex to me is such a primal, heavily-encoded, Darwinianly-supported, neurochemically-reinforced phenomenon, it has to be—which is why we have seven billion people. But I don't think you can stand by and just say...

R: Yeah, don't do that.

G: ... "Don't do that!" and hope you'll get spiritual. It doesn't work that way. Sex is one you've got to go into, feel it, explore it, understand it, touch the depths of it, and you can move on from there. But you can't just do this to sex (*holds hand out*) and keep out of the way. There are things, as we've been saying, that are really more intense than sex.

R: As Gandhi said it too. People were saying "Can I have possessions?" And he would say "Sure. Just renounce the possessor." To really go into sex in the way that you're describing, actually means that asymptotically you're approaching total selflessness.

G: Right.

R: That's where it can be actually part of the tool for going beyond thought.

Religion has failed... now what?

R: One of the memes that I've picked up from you is the idea that religion has failed. Got to let it sit there... a little bit. I've been amazed, as I kind of had a path unfold for me. I wasn't even aware that there was such a thing as a spiritual path, and then I was on one. (*laughs*)

G: (*laughs*) Whoops!

R: It just didn't even exist. I had some ayahuasca experiences, and even then it took many years to realize just what was unfolding for me. Because of that, I then looked at the major religious traditions. I'd already been a meditator, but I thought of that in a very kind of secular way, that I was altering my brain to fire better. When I read that first—or maybe you said it in conversation actually, I don't remember, I thought, "Oh wow! I spent all my life rejecting religion, and then I come around to it, and then it's a failure!" (*laughs*)

G: (*laughs*)

R: The last with the latest, right?

G: Too late!

R: (*Sings*) "It's too late baby!" Yes, so it's interesting, though, to just let it sit there. The failure of religion, the utter and total complete failure, that it's had its turn. By that of course what we mean is large scale, institutional, certified reconnection with our divinity. "Religion", in the etymological sense, means "reconnect". In that sense, it's a great, great attempt over the past couple of thousand years. But maybe we really are in the epoch where it's just got to come down.

G: Nobody, especially religions, wants to hear this, of course. All you have to do is logon and look at what's happening in the world today. It's difficult, from my perspective, to try to argue that in fact the world's better because it has religion right now. The only thing that you can say is, "Well what if it weren't there, it would be a lot worse!"

R: Yes.

G: You say, "Well, how much worse could it be?" Look at what's going on right now in the name of religion, and has gone on for a long time in the name of religion. How many wars were waged back for the last two thousand years over religion of one kind or another, for somebody's cause, against somebody else's cause.

The amount of "civilizing" it has done through its "thou shalts" and "thou shalt nots" and its hierarchy of leaders, you could argue, is tremendously offset by the great evil that's been done in its name. Without that "reason", you could not have done that evil. There's a good book, *Zen at War*, which is really about Buddhism and war, documenting how the Japanese brought in religion, Buddhism. They had Shinto at the time but Buddhism was more useful to them because they could use this to justify their actions. This book has lots of citations—a very carefully researched work. They actually justified their going into the rape of Nanking on that basis that "We did this because we had to. We were saving them from themselves because they were really going the wrong way." This extended up to the forties. They pulled in Buddhism and moved out Shinto as a main powerbase.

Religion has been used so negatively for so long that it's hard to believe we can't find a better system. We've got so much more capability to interact now, that I think that has

154

brought down a lot of barriers that were there before.

R: The question it raises is, "Where are all the awakened people if we've been at this for two thousand, twenty-five hundred or three thousand years?"

G: Yes!

R: But then, because this is a dialogue, what comes up dialogically for a lot of people is—and this is where I was growing up—"a pox on all their houses then!" No religion, right? What's interesting is, "you can't live with it, can't live without it." If we go a little bit slowly and instead of saying, "Okay, well, no religion!" and "It's all been a scam!", you know this is all the grand illusion that it just serves to fatten the coffers of x, y and z—you could say, "Now wait a minute... what about rationalism? What has rationalism done in the past twenty-five hundred years?" It too...

G: Why don't you define that?

R: I'll define rationalism as the belief in human reason and its capacity to manipulate matter in the external world. A lot of times, myself included, we look at the failure of religion and we say "Okay, well that's failed, but the thing that produced my iPhone hasn't." So I'm going to put my belief, knowingly or unknowingly, in that. The problem with that is that there's mission creep on rationalism.

What is rationalism good at? It's good at making iPhones, extracting coal, making cars, manipulating the external world. But except for very specific practices in the wisdom traditions, it's not any good at all at dealing with subjectivity. We can't simply determine from the failure of religion that we ought to become what we would usually call secular. In fact, what it calls forth is a necessity, absolute necessity for individual spiritual responsibility.

G: Yes, well the Communists tried getting rid of religion.

R: Right. Tried to.

G: They tried to stamp out religion but what happened was that one terrible system supplanted another. So it isn't just, as you said, leaving a vacuum behind. Rationalism, as you say, is limited. It can't deal with subjectivity, but secular humanism is emerging on the scene and many people think maybe it's the answer. It's something that I think many people could buy into. We're good at relationships and caring for others in the group as part of our evolutionary make-up—a lot of our brain is developed to do just that. We like groups, so how about a secular humanist group that doesn't have a hierarchy and doesn't impose on me a bunch of haves and have-nots, or dos and don't-dos?

R: Then there's a chicken-egg problem here: in order to establish this hypothetical group of secular humanists who are going to manifest this, let's just call it *compassion*, they're going to have to avoid simply projecting themselves into others. Given the strength of how powerful rationalism is in our culture, we can think that we have a kind of scientific point of view on who that other is.

G: Oh, exactly.

R: And we can't!

G: Right, but we have mirror neurons, whose function it is to make us believe that we can tell from these actions or the voice tone or what their eyes are doing right now...

R: What do you mean by that?! (*laughs*)

G: (*laughs*) Exactly! ... using our mirror neurons we believe we can know what the other person's mind is. In fact, we *can't* know. All we're doing is projecting what we know, and what we know of behaviors from the past, and coming up with some kind of a heuristic: "Oh I think they're thinking 'this'." This is almost always wrong at some level. But at least it's an attempt we have as a social species to try to get across that unbridgeable gap.

R: We're intertwined with each other but we don't experience each other.

G: We can't.

R: Yeah.

G: No, but you can't really know somebody else's mind.

R: Right, so what our hypothetical secular humanists would need as their first principle is that they *don't know*. This is contrary to the usual way we think of secular humanism which was like the renaissance in Europe, when human beings were taking the mantle of responsibility from God or the gods; we're using our capacity for reason and going forward. That was a great run even though it included a lot of the horrors you were talking about before. But now we're at the point where we know so much about the world, we know so much about the cosmos, that we can actually know how limited our knowledge is about them.

We can also know how limited our understanding is of each other. We can know the limits on logic and rationality themselves. It has to be this kind of first principle—that the first principle of the practice of, what we are calling for the moment "secular humanism"—although that's a kind of a target word sometimes for people from the religious right, but you know, we'll come up with a name for it, we're neologistas. The first principle has to be "don't know"... even "dono". We can call it "Donohism".

G: We've talked about this meeting with Peter Senge from MIT next week on this whole organizational restructuring thing, which really operates on the very principle that you get to "don't know" as a group. When you get to "don't know", then in fact something can really flower with that. But we've got to somehow get comfortable with this don't know, and get past believing that we do know when in fact we don't know.

I think one of the useful things of the internet "blah blah" is that we don't know. We can look at this thing and we can say, "My god, the world is complicated! My little tiny space of what I know something about is so small, compared to everything else that's out there!" Then you see, "I really don't know much at all!" I guess Newton is the last person that thought he could know everything, but now there's so much information, in even the tiniest field, that you have to be humbled by that—unless you're tremendously arrogant.

R: So you can know everything there is to know about neuroscience, assuming that for a moment that it's possible, but you can't know about the crossover of neuroscience and K-pop, right?

G: No, no. It's too much.

R: And there's always some convergence that is emerging that is not knowable. Egoically, experientially we're going to experience that as a 'gap', as a lack. We're going to say, "Oh my gosh! Get control of that information!" But the more we can come to see it as a dance we can say, "Oh wow, now look! There's this crossover between how neurons fire listening to music and an analysis of how businesses have exploited that to create the perfect commercial music product."

G: That's right. Yes.

R: We have to bring it back to the sheer pleasure of not knowing.

G: I was working with this one fellow, he was in his twenties, and I asked him, "What do you do these days?" He replied, "Well, I was on YouTube for seven hours!" I said, "What did you find out?" He said, "I don't know!" (laughs)

R: (*laughs*)

G: If you get on there and you see enough stuff, you say "I have no idea what's going on." Because there's so much information that it does humble you very quickly. You know, you just recognize, "I don't what's going on."

R: Then that's where the mindfulness can come in. Because he's saying "Seven hours on YouTube?" It's not really "you", you know! You don't need to take the name of it literally. That's where this sense of, "Who is the one who is watching YouTube?" becomes primary.

That's one of the things that we bracket when we're taking in external information: "Who is taking in that external information?" When I'm able to turn my consciousness around, like when I'm between projects saying, "What should I be working on?" I have tasks that are before me—What should I be working on?, I say "Who's asking?" As soon as I really look and see who's asking, whatever it is I'm supposed to be working on manifests.

So that's the secondary benefit of this "dono", that by disabusing yourself of, "My mission is to deconstruct religious institutions and offer peer-to-peer spiritual development and tools for spiritual responsibility..."

G: (*laughs*) Not so much.

R: (*laughs*) Exactly! But as soon as you turn it around and say, "Well, actually I'm just talking to my friend Gary about what's going on and that's what's interesting, and let's share that..."

G: Yes, and as you know in doing these dialogues, we don't know what we're going to say.

R: I knew you were going to say that! (*laughs*)

G: (*laughs*) We have no idea what we're going to talk about, and yet somehow something comes out that's quasi-coherent.

R: Well, and maybe we can rename "not knowing" in terms of something novel that comes out. It would probably be very useful in organizational terms because, if we consider the mirror neurons, our usual social groups are caught up with thinking they know what's going on within the group, entraining through each other in mirror neurons. It's: "... and then she's going to say this, and I'm going to say that and then blah, blah, blah..." (*pause*) Something else just happened.

G: Yes, except she doesn't. She says something else.

R: Right.

G: Oh! New model, get the model.

R: And then it starts to cascade. Because she thinks "Nine hundred and ninety times out of a thousand he's going to disagree with me, and he just didn't completely, because he didn't do anything at all. What should I do now? I don't know. I-I-I know how to disagree with him back, but maybe we should look into this roller skates idea." (*laughs*)

Something totally—watermelon... something completely out of the ecosystem of thought that you'd been inhabiting before, and then novelty can come forward. So maybe secular humanism needs a new word too. Maybe that's part of the novelty that needs to come with it, but I really think that the phrase "spiritual responsibility" might be part of what has to go along with it, because each of us has to clean up our own mess—individually.

G: Yes, the responsibility part... that's difficult.

R: Too downer?

G: Well, it begs rules.

R: Well, but if you forgive an English professor, if you say "response-ability"...

G: Yes.

R: You need the ability to respond to the spiritual situation.

G: Yes if you parse it that way.

R: Not the "and thou shalt do this, thou shalt…"

G: Be responsible, yes.

R: No it's true, it's a little bit too much like what you would say to a teenager who was about to go out on a date or something, which…

G: Right, but I think you're spot-on about people needing to understand that not knowing is not a bad place. Not knowing is actually a place from which something extraordinary arises. I think that's a whole different spinoff.

R: It's beautiful.

G: Yes.

R: You look at the Grand Canyon and you take it all in and you're just like… blown away. That's the kind of sublime state of not knowing. What is that??

G: We let go into that state. We like that state.

R: Yes, it's beautiful.

G: (*takes a deep breath*)… and we stop, and we don't know, and we like it! Then you can say, "Well, my life could be like that." And I just wait and see that what spontaneously manifests is so much more intuitive, so much more organic than anything I ever could have come up with before.

R: It's funnier too.

G: It's much funnier!

R: Your laughter comes out.

G: Yes, it's a much cooler place to be in.

R: Yes. Highly recommend it.

G: Yes.

Self-inquiry practices on a busy schedule

R: I wrote a book about ecodelics[11] and how important those were to my own path towards awakening beyond thought. In a way those are easier to talk about than the thing that was also very powerful for me, which was a mainstream media fast that I started going on in early November, 2004. I had put an enormous amount of energy into thinking about politics and thinking about the election, and things turned out in a very absurd way from my perspective. In a way it was a great gift because something clicked and just said enough of all that. That is just useless activity you just engaged in.

So I began, in 2004, systematically turning off all of the media streams that I was more or less unconsciously—by which I mean I wasn't aware of how I was doing it— integrating into my life on a regular basis. I would listen to the radio at night before I went to sleep. I would watch the television news and so forth. And I began to systematically just eliminate that from my cognitive diet. I haven't looked at a newspaper since 2004. I catch glimpses of the headlines and so forth. It's very interesting because it's analogous to your experience of being beyond thought. People say, "How will you know what's going on?"

G: Exactly! What if you don't know what's going on?

R: It's really amazing. You know exactly what is going on because nothing is going on!

---

11. *Darwin's Pharmacy: Sex, Plants and the Evolution of the Noosphere,* University of Washington Press, 2011.

G: That's right! And you're there for that. (*laughs*)

R: (*laughs*) I'm very much present for the fact that absolutely nothing has changed! So it's really funny actually. So I wanted to suggest that there's a fantastic practice that you can engage in. When people think that they don't have time for practice— and I'm frequently guilty of this myself, thinking I need to sleep or I need to do this—that every time they go to throw the media switch, or turn on the remote, turn on the radio in their car or listen to something in their ear, instead of throwing that switch, throw the internal switch of self-inquiry, to simply ask themselves, "Who was the one who was about to turn the switch? What was that person, whoever that was, going to learn?" It's quite remarkable because you may find that you incorporate, in fact, hours of practice in self-inquiry in the course of any given day.

You could even turn that radio on then, once you've paused to think about who was turning on the radio, and witness the one who was listening to the radio, and witness the responses that the one who is listening to the radio is having. You can turn this media bandwidth off which otherwise fills our mind with essentially garbage, and makes us want things that we have no need for obviously, otherwise it wouldn't exist as an industry. It makes us focus our awareness on things that have absolutely no impact on the world.

It's a ridiculous world view to think that if you spend even fifteen minutes a day wondering about media and current events it has anything to do with anything. From a certain perspective, astrology makes more sense than paying attention to what the Republicans or the Democrats are doing. So, I just want to suggest that, as a practice, whenever you go to throw the media switch, throw the self-inquiry switch. I have found that it feels like I have an enormous amount more of time in a day. I'm still busy but it doesn't feel like I'm buffeted by messages constantly.

G: Yes, that's a great practice. That's the nice thing about this self-inquiry practice; you don't have to sit in a room for a long time quietly. It's useful if you can, but if you don't have time to do it or think you don't have time to do it (you do, you just think you don't), then create some "triggering" event. You used media access as a great one because you're very present for that. But it can be going to the bathroom, getting a cup of tea, answering the phone, answering email, texting …

Pick some triggering event that will prompt you to take this much time just to ask, "Who is it that's going to do this?" Or, "Where am I, this one right now who wants to get a cup of tea?" or whatever it is. That's just enough break. The big thing is to not let this internal stream go sixteen or seventeen hours a day, but break it here and there. Muslims do this five times a day—perform the *salat* to Mecca. That's a very powerful practice. Stop your day for a few minutes and focus on yourself, the eternal, the divine. It makes a big, big difference in how your day runs. This self-inquiry process that we do is very amenable to that. You can do it any place. In fact, it's better done when reaching for the media because that's where you're seeing yourself doing an action. You can say, "Oh, who is doing that?" It's very powerful, and very accessible.

R: What's interesting is that once we start doing it, maybe not exactly right away but it seems like right away, you feel something happen. If you say, "Who is drinking this tea right now? Who is speaking right now?" Just turn your awareness around and actually look and see. You get this feeling, and maybe the feeling is just a release of that other version of yourself, maybe it's something else, I can't say; everybody has to find out for themselves. But there is this feeling that if there was a drug that delivered that feeling regularly with no side-effects over the course of a day, you would be going to it like a rat in a lab maze. That is what I find that happens. You start pausing, asking yourself, "Who is doing this?" Then you feel like I'm feeling right now and you say, "Oh I think I'll remember to do that again." (*laughs*)

G: The thing that people get confused about is that they think there's an answer. They say, "I ask 'Where am I?' and it gets very quiet. It's very still. There's no answer there!" I say, well duh! That's the answer! The answer is, there's nothing there. But that "nothing there", if you keep doing it, keep going back to it, the space gets more accessible, it gets larger, stays longer, gets sweeter. You just keep going back again and again and again.

We believe that each time we go back, and the brain sees that clear space, it says "Whoa! What's that? That's really cool, let's do that!" If you give it enough of those spaces, the brain has time to re-functionalize, and it will. It will select a different functional pattern if it gets enough of those data points so that it can do the re-functionalizing. That's all you have to do, just keep asking, watching for that space, looking for something that doesn't have an answer. "Where am I? I can't find myself any place." "Where am I? I'm here talking all day long to myself, I must be here someplace!" You stopped. Then you go back to your work. The brain had a break there. You broke your stream of thoughts, and now your brain has some data to work with.

R: If you work in computer or technology support, most of the time what you go through, if you're doing best practices, is to call up somebody. They say okay and… what is the first thing that they tell you to do?

G: Turn it off.

R: Just turn the damn thing off for a second… (*laughs*)

G: (*laughs*) Exactly!

R: Turn it back on. "Heyyyy that worked!" But we haven't made the next step. We're this highly technological society and we should say, "'Wow what incredible grace there is in just turning something off for a moment and then letting it come back on." My best analogy is that I probably went through forty years without a significant reboot. There's all this garbage that takes up all this code that accumulates that you need to get rid of, viruses that need to be buffed out. If you just start doing that a little bit during the day, every day, then the day never really becomes a day in an interesting way.

G: It's like forty days. If you do the reboot forty times a day then the whole thing changes... I call computer support... "I have an enormous problem, a horrendous mess here! What should I do?" Turn it off. (*laughs*)

R: Sir, there's something on the computer called a switch, you might... (*laughs*)

G: Just turn it off! Just turn it off! (*laughs*) It comes back up again. Like you say, you accumulate all kinds of garbage on your machine, and you accumulate all kinds of garbage on this machine.

R: Oh yes, how could you not?

G: So if you could just stop, open up the space, reboot, then the whole thing gets fresh again.

R: Yes, and it's beautiful because then, what I meant before by saying a day no longer becomes a day, is that then you experience the day as an almost infinite series of qualitatively distinct moments. It's not like you get on this train of, "Ohhhh, this is a bad day!" or, "Ohhhh, this is a good day!" Either one is a problem because then it all becomes this one thing. Whereas if you have these discrete moments, you feel these qualitative differences throughout the day and the day feels subjectively, in a good way, like forever!

G: You aren't dragging around something that happened four hours ago.

R: What? When was that? That was an eon ago!

G: Exactly! Exactly, because each time you reboot you stop the stream of obsessing about whatever it was that happened four hours ago that you just can't get out of your mind. You just stop, just give it a break. It's, "Whoa..." And often, not always but often, it will fall away. Then something else will start over the next period. Each time you break, like you eloquently say, it's a bunch of periods that all sequence out.

R: One of the misconceptions that I always had is that once I start doing this all the time then bad stuff will stop happening! And of course, that's not the case at all. So maybe I open an email and it's work-related and I go grrrrr! But the point is that then I reboot just as I start feeling it, asking, "Who's having this emotion? Who's having this feeling?" Maybe I feel it for a little while, but it goes away much more quickly than before.

Before, if something would happen in the morning, then it would happen all day long... I'd feel it all day long. I'd be teaching and feeling it while I was teaching. Then I'd come home and I'd talk to my wife about it and maybe the response was adequate or the response was not adequate. I'd been completely wronged in this email and why couldn't she see that I'd been completely wronged? Instead you just turn it off, and okay there was that moment and now there is this other moment.

A friend of mine did something the other day and he felt bad about it. He said "God, you know I just... it's like I don't know. How can I make that right?" And he said, "Is there a way I can make that right?" And I said, "Yeah, sure." He said, "What's that?" And I said, "Just let go of it." (*laughs*)

G: (*laughs*) Problems don't get better by aging. You have got to somehow terminate that process.

R: Yes, you just let go of it. It's in the past. It doesn't even exist anymore. It's no longer real. It's a fantasy about something that may have happened.

G: That's right. Which you can't change. That's why they call it the "past" because it is past and you can't go back again, so let go of it.

R: Yes. Fortunately.

Sleep

R: We've talked about the necessity of physical practice, and a rather obvious one, but one that poses a widespread difficulty in our society—because we're such a highly mediated society and we have amazing things like electric lights and so forth which artificially alter our relationship to sunlight and darkness—is sleep. And if I know that I'm not getting enough sleep, then there's no feeling of connection with pure consciousness.

G: Right.

R: So I was wondering if we could maybe talk a little bit about different practices besides the obvious one which is to get as much sleep as you need, no more no less. What are some techniques that you have found to be useful?

G: One thing that many people find useful is to establish a pre-sleeping routine to establish cues that the body recognizes. Every night I do a little posture flow and a little *pranayama*, a breathing practice. It takes 10 or 15 minutes. Then the brain knows, "okay we're going to sleep now." It's done this enough times that the brain recognizes it. So that's been very important to training the brain into sleeping now.

For me, a lot depends upon what I eat and when I eat it, too. If I eat protein very late that's not a good thing. Carbs late, protein midday or so. I try not to eat very late. If I'm eating at 10 o'clock at night it's not going to be a good night's sleep. I don't drink very much alcohol, but when I do, it doesn't take much to upset my sleep. So I try to drink as little alcohol as possible, eat carbohydrates late and not protein, and try to get some exercise. If you get some exercise late in the day, in my experience, say 5 to 8 o'clock, it makes sleeping much easier.

R: As I tend to go to sleep about 10:30 or 11:00, my routine seems to stem from about 8 o'clock onward, giving cues to the brain to set it up for sleep. It can actually extend backwards in time further than I expected because with hindsight I can see that I have trouble sleeping on the days when I was doing something different between 8:00 and 10:00—not giving my brain the right cues.

G: Exactly. Right.

R: Now, it feels like that's good guidance and sometimes we do these things intuitively, but I think it's good to be aware also that we can set up a practice whereby we're more likely to get good sleep. But then there's the kind of next level where, you're on a plane or you find yourself awake, unable for some reason to actually fall asleep at night. I have found *ad hoc* meditative techniques to be very helpful for that. What I used to do all the time is that my default mode network would be going, worrying about not sleeping.

G: Yes. Stories about not sleeping.

R: Oh my god, and then this is going to happen... and then oh... ! You know? So I think again it's obvious but it's worth remembering, that these techniques—of self-inquiry, for example—can be very useful for any brief episodes of sleeplessness that I have experienced where I can turn my consciousness around and say, "Who's not sleeping?"

And then sometimes when I'm turning my consciousness around and saying who's not sleeping, I say, "Am I loving God with all of my heart?" since that's one of my inquiry practices. When I do that it can be a very beautiful energetic meditative space where I'm really neither asleep nor awake and I pass sort of imperceptibly into sleep. In the meantime I have this very energizing and beautiful experience of a kind of non-dual state. It becomes a kind of opportunity for practice. As I mentioned to you before, a couple of nights ago I woke up at 4:00 am and of course that's the classic hour for meditation, so maybe that's a clue from my practice, "Hey, get up and meditate!" Right?

G: Yes, as we've talked before, the brain, after a while on the path, begins to take control of this process. Once the "I" gets small enough, the brain is really driving the bus. If it doesn't get enough processing time, my experience and that of many people I've worked with, is that you'll find yourself awake in the middle of the night, 4 o'clock in the morning or something. There's actually a name for that 4-6 in the morning period, because it's such a special, powerful time—*Pratha Kala* or *Brahma Muhoortham*. You find yourself awake. The brain's saying, "Look, just go and sit someplace, be quiet, be still, don't do anything, we just need some time here. It's not about you, it's about work we have to do."

R: Yes.

G: So you find yourself sitting in the middle of the night, just sitting there quietly—and you don't know what's going on. Something is happening... the brain's working "offline" re-patterning, re-functionalizing. Just be present for that as you will likely run into it. Almost everybody experiences this as they get on down the path as the brain wants more processing time. It loves this space, wants to get into it as much as it can and wants to stay there for as long as it possibly can. So it'll wake you up to do that.

R: What I've found is that when the brain does that, when it wakes whoever this is up, and says, "Hey!" that there's not really a deficit of sleep. My resistance is sometimes saying, "Oh well if I get up now, I'm going to be tired." But if I just

172

get up and meditate, or even meditate in bed which might work contra to the cues that we were talking about earlier, then inevitably there's about half an hour or so of meditation, and then sleep comes and it's no issue. It's as if I had never awakened during the night at all.

G: That's right.

R: Whereas if you don't accept that and fight it and try to get back to sleep, then there can be issues.

G: I have a blog post on sleep. We know enough about sleep patterns to know that you need to go 35-40 minutes to get effective sleep. But getting up and doing a practice for 35 or 40 minutes, and then coming back to bed, often works really well. Lying in bed, in my experience, hoping it's going to get better, doesn't usually work as well.

R: Yes.

G: Get up, do the meditation, and then come back to bed.

R: I found that sometimes it works but sometimes it doesn't. When it works in bed it really is quite delicious. It's just a different mode of meditation really.

G: Yes. There's a simple but powerful thing you can do if you wake up in the middle of the night with this wild mind going on: remember the old Zen quote about "Breath sweeps mind." Just go back into your breath with long, slow, smooth breaths, and focus on your exhales. It sounds too simple, but it is really powerful. Just keep going back into your breath and long slow exhales, and you'll be surprised how much that will slow down or stop the narrative mind, and perhaps get you back to sleep.

R: (*snore*)

Spiritual practice with partner/wife/family as Zen masters

R: Let's talk about the role of family in practice. Probably most of us are not living in situations where everybody in the family is on the same page in terms of practice that can...

G: We aren't monks either.

R: We're not monks, and we value our work in the world. But one of the last big challenges that many people face as they're withering their narrative mind is how to deal with that narrative mind in the context of family... taking care of the kids, making sure the spouse is happy and so forth. Apropos our other discussion, how is it that we can work with that to make it a really productive platform for awakening? The way in which I see it happening a lot of times is that people start to resent or distance themselves from their family and feel like, "Oh I need to go to a monastery!" or something, rather than seeing that actually right here is maybe some of our most important practice.

G: Yes, in different guises, whether you're married or not married or whatever that means to you, it comes up a lot. A long-term partner will have discovered over the course of years how to push every button that you have. Nobody knows you as well as your kids or your partner does. They do know how to wound you, and you them, over the course of time. It can be a very difficult thing to unwind yourself from and keep your process moving forward.

I know in my case they're very powerful teachers—my kids and my wife have been very strong teachers. None of them are really into this, and so that creates some friction and some chances for misunderstanding, but there's no stronger Zen master than your kids or your wife to point out to you where you really do need to do work. If you go to *sesshin* or something, a Zen retreat where you spend 7 or 8 days with somebody, and he shouts at you for 7 days, he doesn't have any idea exactly where you are compared to what your kids and your spouse do. So, they're very valuable teachers.

R: I always found that to be the case. Something that came up for me, that I really had to work through, was the distinction between love and attachment. The challenge that I continually faced was that it felt as though the love I have for my family meant that I was attached to them—that love and attachment were hand in hand.

I felt the need for some particular outcome. I felt that there needed to be a narrative that meshes for all of them, so that my story matches my wife's story, matches my kids' story. It seems so completely obviously true when you're inside a family context, precisely because in order for there to be that long term relationship, we've learned about those buttons and how to push them. So what you're doing is you're all evolving stories that allow you to push each other's buttons in different orders and then sometimes the pushing of the buttons wounds more than it should, right?

I found then that the distinction between love and attachment was very helpful. I realized that what I was thinking of as love was as much attachment as it was love, where love is actually the surrender of the personal narrative in the context of the other as opposed to the imposition of the personal narrative.

This probably happened 4 or 5 years ago but I'm still working it through. But it remains useful for me to ask myself, query myself and say, "Am I acting out of attachment or am I acting out of love? Am I feeling attachment or am I feeling love?" The more I do it, the more I see that that kind of letting go happens much more quickly, even in a few seconds. It has given me a supplemental method of self-inquiry because it allows a particular phrasing to look back and see, "How am I encountering this? Who is encountering this?" If there's somebody there that has a story about how this needs to go, then that's...

G: That's something to work on.

R: It's distressing to think that the letting go, the undermining of the narrative status quo, is also going to undermine any loving connection. But the opposite is true—as we've discussed—because the attachment is actually *hiding* the love that is there. The love has given rise to the attachment in a certain way. The "I" comes in and wants to direct the love—because love is scary to the "I". But when you can wither the attachment, more love can manifest. Then you end up more or less just being there for the other person. It can be painful sometimes if you can see the way in which the other person or persons are not so much there.

G: Right.

R: That itself can present its own challenges. Another "A" word comes up and it's acceptance. That as the attachment withers and the love grows, not only is love conducive to a kind of surrender of the personal narrative, love is also conducive to acceptance. That that's just how he or she is and who they are and no amount of my creation of a story about them and how they need to change is going to affect that. The miracle is that as soon as you stop trying to impose change on them and you just accept them for who they are, and don't react to their buttons or try to push their buttons, there's movement.

G: Yes. As we've talked, it can be difficult at first. If you've lost attachment, there's less and less of a "you" there, an "I" there, then what happens is that you won't be responding to the buttons the same way you used to. That can be disconcerting for the relationship, because they're used to having you react in a certain way to certain stimuli. If you've been together a long time, that's a very well established pattern. This isn't written down, but it is there. They know the program and you know the program, so those programs are running and if you don't respond the way you're supposed to then it's "What's wrong? What am I doing wrong that's happening in the relationship now because he isn't responding the way he used to respond?"

In fact, if you keep that space, as you know, if you just keep coming from that space, then your other person will learn, in fact, that the old buttons, the old algorithms don't work anymore, so something's changed here. Then there's a possibility for something dynamic happening, not by you telling them to change, but just by their recognizing that the game has changed. Then they will find themselves looking internally, and not because you tell them, "You should do this, be more spiritual..."

R: Watch my video! (*laughs*)

G: Watch my video! (*laughs*) But they will find that they're moving to a different space as well.

R: Yes.

G: The worst thing you can do in my experience is to prose-lytize or tell them, "You should be like me..." It just doesn't work that way. That's the last thing that's effective. You've got to be very still yourself. The more quiet you get and the less attached you are, as you were saying, the more chance there is for them to begin to understand themselves and learn their way out of the algorithms that they've been using, that we helped them create.

R: At first, as you mentioned, for quite some time, when the buttons are pushed and it doesn't work then, they're pushed again and again, and maybe the buttons are pushed with more intensity. It's like people on an elevator (*pushing buttons madly*) "It's not here yet!"...

G: Exactly! (*laughs*)

R: And so...

G: Push it ten times and make it come faster.

R: That is a real teaching. Maybe you've withered your self, cultivated your self-inquiry enough, so you are not reacting. The button's pushed, pushed again and again. It's a gift because then you find there's your limit. It got pushed again, or it got pushed exactly at the right time or in this sequence with these other buttons. It's as if you're being given the wiring diagram for your own emotional attachments. You can see it, you can feel the shock. Then that's, again, a gift. This is why, at least in my experience, the best progress comes not from leaving society and going into seclusion, but by being with the challenges of everyday life, which really can be the best teachers of all, as you've said. I've experienced that.

G: One of J Krishnamurti's quotes that I like is that you only see yourself in relationship. Virginia Woolf famously said, as you know, that we have as many "I's" as we have relationships. So your situation is such that you are put face to face with those relationships. You get to understand facets of yourself because different "I's" show up for each relationship and those will unwind separately. You will begin to see that in fact they are not glued together as one thing, they really are relationship-indexed.

R: So, at some level at least, you have to unwind each of them independently. There is not just the deconstruction of the "I", because the "I" emerges as different facets of what you are in relation with all the different kinds of experiences and worlds that you dwell in.

G: Right. It's very helpful to see that in fact I am several different relationships. There is not one "I" there, you can just see the "I" change each time. It's why we do this "When am I?" exercise. You look and say, "Well, I'm one person here, one person there, one person..." There is no continuity to this "I", it's just an *ad hoc* entity that comes racing in for that particular relationship. As you change, as your "I" gets unwound or the base gets unwound, the relationships change, necessarily.

You do get to see the other person maybe for the first time in a long, long time; with no attachment—I know you've seen this as well. You just see them as somebody else, not just trying to get through the day, but somebody else trying to live their life as best they can. They're really struggling to do that and you're struggling too and so you watch that. You say, "Ohhh..." Now you begin to get real empathy for the other person, with no attachment, just clear seeing that, in fact, I see them for the beauty that they are, with no judgment.

R: And you see them as aspects of the One that you're discovering.

G: Right, exactly.

The difference between pain and suffering...

R: Let's talk about physical pain and its source.

G: Oh, oh, yes, physical pain.

R: "Can getting to no thoughts help with physical pain? And if so, how?" This is what a couple of people have asked and I wonder if people who've seen some of the videos might get the sense that what we're talking about is mind as distinct from the body, rather than body-mind.

G: It's important to make a distinction between pain and suffering. "Pain" remains as you don't lose any of your nerve endings. That isn't the plan. You want to have those to protect the body; you don't want to burn your finger continuously in the fire. So we keep that pain part.

What we can ameliorate and go after is the "suffering" part, which is the story I make in my mind about "pain". We've all been there. You have all kinds of projections, memories from the past, projections about how horrible it's going to be in the future. "Is this pain ever going to end?" "Why me?" All of those stories come in and you can just not have those. If you don't have those stories, then you're just left with the pure pain. That may be very difficult but it's nothing compared to what you can create as far as suffering in your mind.

R: That distinction between pain and suffering is very useful because obviously there are many different kinds of pain. There are people who have to deal with horrible chronic pain on an everyday basis. There are brief outbursts of pain that we can experience in our everyday life. What I have observed is that even in those brief outbursts of pain being able to turn the consciousness back towards its source allows for an "at once" detachment from the pain and a kind of sharing of the pain with the whole cosmos, right? You're not carrying it all yourself.

It's worth noting what I've observed in my own life, which is that this, in itself, can be actually very healing. You're absolutely right about this distinction between pain and suffering. No, you're not going to be able to prevent the physical events of pain—we're all going to face those at different moments. But as we wither the narrative mind there's less of a person there to narrate the pain into suffering, as you put it.

But then what's interesting is that that's a kind of snapshot. Okay I'm riding my bicycle up a very steep hill for the first time, and I'm able to be in Source so the pain is there but the suffering… not so much. What's very interesting is that means that I can keep riding up that hill, and in keeping riding up that hill and other hills, then I can get stronger. So, in fact, it doesn't even hurt me riding up that hill now. That's a positive version of it, but there's also what I experienced from long term allergic inflammation both in my lungs and on my skin. When you can make the distinction between pain and suffering, the pain itself starts to wither.

When it comes to things like inflammation, if you can get some distance on it, you can tend it better. You stop thrashing around quite so much because pain makes us all terrible caretakers of ourselves. Then that leads to the decrease of the inflammation a little bit, and the next time, and the next time, to the point that, almost paradoxically, now I do experience suffering sometimes because I feel so well most of the time; then something happens and I go (*gasp*) "What's that?" I have a moment that I have to get some distance on.

So I think that making a distinction between pain and suffering is fundamental, and there can be a feedback loop towards experiencing real healing by making that distinction between pain and suffering.

G: There were some studies on what's the best way to ameliorate your pain[12]... do this to it (*push away*) or move into it? Consistently they show that you should not try to wall off your pain and insulate yourself from it. You're better off to open up to it, face into it and be one with it.

I wrote a blog post on the placebo effect, which really turns out to be a very high bar. We're finding out now why pharmaceutical companies have a very difficult time beating the placebo effect. So you can do it all yourself, and the mind is not passive in this placebo effect. The mind has the ability to fix itself if you just let it—get out of the way, stop turning it into suffering, let the mind/brain operate and work with pain, then it can be really very effective.

They've also found that there is a thing called "placebo analgesia". When you're in this "not suffering" mode, but you're just attending to the pain—there is an analgesic effect. It seems to work, not unlike an aspirin, and actually cuts down the pain, and your perception of pain. From that perspective there's so much we can do if we just get out of the suffering and be present for what the pain is, where it is and what's going on there.

R: That feeds into accepting that the world is perfect, because nothing can seem to be a clearer signal that the world is not perfect than when we're experiencing pain. But, as you point out, if we then go, "Oh, this needs to go away!"... we make that separation, that dualism, that it exacerbates it. But if we can be with the pain, as difficult as it is, even for a moment, then that pain... remains pain rather than suffering, and it does feel experientially like that analgesic effect is real. So

---

12. *The Meaning and Process of Pain Acceptance*, Diane LaChapelle, Susan Lavoie, and Ainsley Boudreau, Pain Res Manag. 2008 May-Jun; 13(3): 201–210.

we're not just talking about the mind, we're talking about the body-mind, because the mind and the body can't be separated from each other.

G: Right, right.

The "I" can't dance

R: Is there a qualitative difference, particularly in the beginning, if you practice meditation with others as well as solo? Do you have experience with that, or have a neuroscientific perspective on that?

G: Neuroscience is pretty lean on that. It's common experience, even in the Bible. You know the quote, "Where two or more are gathered together in my name, then therefore am I also there". So that experience holds true. Almost everybody feels that something happens when you get into a group. If you get in a group of four, five, six, seven... then the energy changes.

We've talked a lot about energy coherence and about how that changes when you get out of the way and there's less of an "I" there. What manifests is different as you're more in alignment with other people who are not so much there, as an "I". That seems to feed upon itself... it gets stronger and much clearer in my experience.

R: It really does. It feels like, on the one hand, particularly when one is starting practice, that it's good to have that sort of routine where other people are going to be there. So, I'll do that. But I think it's also, as you said, that there's something qualitative that happens when a group forms.

There's not much research on the science of meditation 'together'. It feels like there's something that is enabled, or even catalyzed, in the context of the non-dual experience, by being with multiple players as it were. When I sit down and there's somebody sitting next to me and we get still and silent together, it somehow doesn't encourage this idea of "I am meditating now," as opposed to "There is meditating occurring in all directions here." It's almost as if there is an energetic reaction between us in which the whole is more than the sum of the parts. At least on an intuitive and experiential level it's really something worth encouraging—that getting together actually potentiates the non-dual experience as well as solitude.

G: Yes. I think back to the times I sat in Zen *sesshins* where there can be 20, 30, 40, 50 people, and you sit virtually all day long for five, six, seven, maybe 10 days, except for meals and little tasks, and you really do become one. First time, first day, is like (grumble) trying to get yourself positioned and everything, and assessing what this environment's like. By the second or third day, you are one entity just meditating together. It really does work that way. You used the words "sustaining somebody else". If somebody has a problem, then you can feel a break in the energy of the group, and then the group that you're meditating with, kind of pulls them along— keeps them on track. You get really entrained on a long sit with the same person always sitting next to you and you both are meditating as one thing. There's a sense of that not being two people anymore.

R: Right. So for example, in one of the legal ayahuasca churches in Brazil, the Santo Daime, a good deal of the ceremony is a kind of collective dancing where you're precisely entraining each other into one macro movement together. I do think that something analogous is going on in meditation, that the dance in silence, as it were, is being potentiated in each other so that even if you maybe fall off for a second and you start to go in your head, "Oh… does it mean anything that I'm a Scorpio?", and then it's almost as if there's a kind of collective silence that holds you together.

G: Yes. The dance metaphor that we use all the time works for this. My most recent book, *Dancing Beyond Thought*, to which you wrote the foreword, is very much like that. You're dancing together and you can watch the syncopation, you are matching beats, moving rhythmically together. That's very much a part of what we're talking about here: meditation with others becomes a dance.

Your life becomes a dance, just as the meditation with others becomes a dance where everything goes along synchronously. If you get asynchronous with the dance, then it doesn't work so well. Then you get the, "Oh, she's a lot better than I am" and the dance breaks down. As long as you stay out of the "I" then it becomes a beautiful synchronous dance or meditation, and your life is as well.

R: Right. And the "I" can't dance.

G: No, the "I" can't dance! "I's" just cannot dance.

R: If the "I" tries to dance it doesn't give up enough of its control in order to "be with" the other dancers. It's just asserting itself.

G: Just even watching typical social dancers...

R: I'd rather not, but go ahead.

G: Same thing happens when you're out there and everybody's really into the music and they're really not into themselves. It's a beautiful thing... The group can really move together. If somebody goes to, "Oh she's a lot better than I am!", "She's not as good as I am!", "He's really a klutz over there!" Then you can watch folk lose track of the syncopation, go out of the rhythm and out of the dance because they've become an "I" identifying with a story that doesn't play into the dance.

R: With that typical social dancing, there often comes the need to individuate and assert control.

G: Yes.

R: When you meditate collectively, when you're doing the silent dance of meditation together, any need to control or bring the "I" into it feels wrong. You feel yourself falling off as opposed to being in that kind of very sweet and solid space of this collective silent energy.

G: With our neurochemistry, we do know that dopamine and endogenous opioid levels increase as you get more meditative and become more aligned with Source. The brain so likes this still space that it supports it neurochemically and leaving it is not only disharmonious but really unpleasant. It's an unpleasant effort to move out of that deep stillness—we become locked into it.

R: Right, so the "I" shows up to punch its card, "Okay I'm on duty now", and you're like, "No, no... fizzbo."

G: "Are you still around?"

R: And, "Weren't you fired a long time ago? You're still showing up but you have nothing else to show up for."

G: "We gave you the slip."

R: Apparently not. So it does feel like a beautiful thing to meditate together and this sense of collective entrainment is really something worth pursuing. Whenever we feel like we're manifesting ourselves as "I am meditating" we can practice saying, "meditation is happening."

G: Right.

The Neuroscience of non-dual awakening

R: Science.

G: Science.

R: Yes, you know, this is usually thought of as a sacred spiritual religious path, but science has been very useful for your practice. It's also been useful for mine. I thought it would be useful talking about the sort of uses and abuses of science for the awakened life as it were.

G: Yes, when I was starting, way back when pterodactyls flew in the air, way back...

R: Yes, I've seen those pictures.

G: We had no science of the brain. There just wasn't anything. We had some really clumsy EEG stuff but nobody ever paid any attention to it, and there was nothing to go on. So you just kind of flew around in the dark. As an empirical scientist, I thought we should have a science about this thing. Didn't matter, we didn't have one so we just kept trying things and stuff worked out.

R: Flying blind.

G: Flying blind. But now in the last ten years, maybe less, eight years... we really do now have a lot of science that gives great insights into what has been happening. What happened with psychedelics, how it looks like in meditation, how meditation develops, how much time it takes to change things, what centers are being affected. We still have a long ways to go. There'll be much more in the future to come out of this. There are some very good people, lots of funding coming into it and top peer-reviewed journals. But the science has really been fantastic.

R: I've always been fascinated by science and at the same time skeptical about it. That's what it really means to be into science: to be skeptical of any particular scientific claim. I really got down and looked at some of the studies that you mentioned to me, and I found that they pointed to the fact that there actually is such a thing as a non-dual state. That the non-dual state correlates with different kinds of empirical data. That doesn't mean that the empirical data tells us what the non-dual state is... there is a long history of reports that there is a state where you experience your non-separation from all things and the silencing of the mind and the emptying of images in the mind—the inference being that that state is to be sought after. By whom, of course is a good question. The fact that we have correlative data, that says "Yes, maybe..." even if that's all it says is, "Yes maybe", then it's not all pie in the sky, it's not a UFO. The non-dual state that we're describing here actually can be modeled scientifically. To me that's huge.

G: We know about the Default Mode Network[13] which really is the key to understanding this. We know there are the two sub-networks, one of which is "yourself in time", and the other

13. The default mode network is an interconnected and anatomically defined brain system that preferentially activates when individuals engage in internal tasks such as daydreaming, envisioning the future, retrieving memories, and gauging others' perspectives. It is negatively correlated with brain systems that focus on external visual signals... Activity in the network negatively correlates with activity in regions involved in attention and executive function. In humans, the default mode network has been hypothesized to generate spontaneous thoughts during mind-wandering.

one is "you and others". The traditional mystical experiences are "no sense of personal time", i.e. "now, now, now", and "no sense of anything other than yourself", i.e. "All is One". You can actually look in that network and see how those things are coded in and what centers need to be shut down to make that situation happen. Whether it's psychedelics or meditation, we know what centers code in for that.

R: So the one network points to the fact that this is an experiential reality, just as real as my experience that your shirt is black, that it's all one thing. I find it intriguing that you pointed in the past to the idea that one of the real quick heuristic devices you can use to identify how far along somebody is on awakening is, do they think they're in control? If you think on that one domain, the "I" in time, it says, "Well of course I'm in control, I'm moving through time as an 'I'." But it's a case of "not so much" when you're in the other domain; it's not a matter of not being in control—more that the question doesn't even make any sense, because what would I be in control of? I am all of this stuff manifesting together. I just think this might be helpful because it doesn't feel like a loss. It doesn't feel like, "Oh, once upon a time there was control where that network of my 'I' was traveling through time and now I no longer have control!" It's more that the whole question of control appears as a kind of non sequitur because that state that had formerly been sort of dominating my experience, which is the "I" traveling through time, and not having enough of it, fades in favor of the sense of self being intertwined or entangled with absolutely everything. So that is very beautiful confirming data. Again, how it works for me is as, "Hey! I'm not nuts"… about that. (*laughs*)

G: (*laughs*)… about that!

R: Exactly. I have experiences which make me look round and say, "How can this be so? What's happening?" And these correspond to experiences reported in the mystical traditions. Now that we have the beginnings of a science, an understanding about the relation between the brain and these "states"—for people who have not had the experience I can say, "You know actually you might have doubts about Sasquatch, you might have doubts about aliens, maybe you don't, maybe you do. But *this* is as much of a reality in the world as oxygen." That to me is huge.

G: Yes, and the whole thing about this, and this is anthropological now, is knowing that roughly 75,000 years ago we created an "I". We did not have one when we broke off from the chimpanzees six million years ago…

R: What are you working on back there?! He's been in the garage all day!

G: (*laughs*) Exactly, but then…

R: This is my creation!

G: Not till 75,000 years ago did we actually evolve this whole construct of a symbolic logic consciousness with an "I" in it. This is a relatively recent invention that we've adaptively developed; it's not something that we had six million years, or even one million, years ago. It's very recent…

R: Right, from an evolutionary perspective 75,000 years is like zero.

G: Nothing, out of six million years when we broke off from the other primates… nothing, it means nothing. Also, you mentioned not being in control. I fell into not having any "free will", because there was no "I" there, and it was like, "Duh, there's nobody there, this isn't even a question anymore." Back to your point… It was also very helpful to see when the science started to roll out, trying to find…

R: Whew!

G: Yes, whew, where the "I" is, we can't find it, it's all over the place. We can look in a hundred places. It's just an *ad hoc* entity. We have the famous Libet experiments[14] where we look and see, "Okay, when do we know we're going to do something, when do we do something, and when does the brain do it?" The brain always starts the whole process. It's now been almost forty years and we've not contradicted that finding.

R: I don't like that.

G: People don't like that!

R: No. "I" don't like that (*laughs*).

G: (*laughs*) There's a great YouTube video out on BBC[15] at a German Institute where they took a reporter in, put him in the machine, looked at him and, lo and behold, the scientist could tell him 6-8 seconds before he goes to do something that in fact this is what he's going to do... left hand, right hand, left hand, right hand. The BBC reporter is just blown away; it's incontrovertible. It's been done over and over and over again. People don't like the answer. They fought against it. They argued against it. Libet even tried to find a way out of it. But it's held up.

R: Indeed they were determined to fight against it.

G: Absolutely.

---

14. "Libet's experiments demonstrated that the unconscious electrical processes in the brain called readiness potential precede conscious decisions to perform volitional, spontaneous acts, implying that unconscious neuronal processes precede and potentially cause volitional acts which are retrospectively felt to be consciously motivated by the subject." This has been demonstrated consistently in many subsequent studies with different study designs and equipment.

15. "Neuroscience and Free Will BBC Video" @ www://youtube/ -i3AiOS4nCE?list=FLMSnyxnteEx7IOPIFkfh3og

R: They couldn't but fight against it (*laughs*).

G: They couldn't but fight against it, yes (*laughs*).

R: This raises the possibility, though, there's also a junk science. In another video we were talking about Suzanne Segal[16] and now there's a new book on depersonalization syndrome. Medicine and the current version of the DSM [Diagnostic and Statistical Manual of Mental Disorders] are ready, willing and able to provide diagnoses, and it raises something interesting… that people can go to their doctors and they say, "Doctor, can you please do a test on my "I"? Can you please locate my "I"? No, no, no, not this one (*points to right eye*). Not this one either (*points to left eye*). Please locate and describe the nature of my "I". Now until they can do that, what sense does it make to talk about depersonalization syndrome? There has to be something there to be lost. If we can maintain our skepticism, particularly towards those models that already mesh well with the kind of psycho-therapeutic establishment that really wants to diagnose us, if we can keep our skepticism, as we learn the scientific models because that's how we learn about them, that's incredibly useful.

G: One of the pushbacks I get back on my science-oriented meditation stuff is, "The problem with you science guys is it always keeps changing. You came up with something five years ago. You thought that was the answer, now you've changed your story. Now you've got a new story. Why should I bother to listen to you because it keeps changing?" My response has been, "Well, four hundred years ago the Catholic Church disciplined Galileo because he kept claiming that the Earth was not the center of the universe, and after four hundred years they admitted they were wrong". So if you want certainty, you can go to the religions and they can give you certainty. It may be incorrect, but it is certain. The thing about science, to the

16. Segal, S (1996). *Collision with the Infinite: A Life Beyond the Personal Self*. San Diego, Calif: Blue Dove Press. ISBN 1-884997-27-9.

best of our abilities, this is the most correct information we have at the moment. When we get better skills in the future, new understandings, then things will change. But it's the best game going.

R: Well, because it can be falsified.

G: Absolutely, you can falsify it.

R: The analogy we were working with before is, if it's wrong and it gets into the Encyclopedia Britannica, it's in there. But if it's on Wikipedia, which is more the "scientific level" in that it can be changed, then it can get better. Does it get better quickly enough and uniformly in all domains? No. But can it change? Absolutely.

G: Well that was one of the early raps against Wikipedia as you can recall. "Oh, it's changing all the time and you can't believe this thing! Go to the Britannica, I can look it up in Britannica. I know what the answer is!" Well, that was the answer ten years ago, but it may not be the answer today.

R: No, it's not the answer.

G: Even about history, we've learned so much about history.

R: In fact even the Wikipedia page on Encyclopedia Britannica has probably changed today (*laughs*).

G: (*laughs*)

R: To its benefit! So I feel like we're such a polarized society about science and religion. Everybody just needs to take it a little bit lighter, and say, "Hey, this could be interesting. This could be useful." Not like, we've proven once and for all—period. What we're looking for is guidance. In terms of the use and abuse of science, the usefulness is, is it a guide? The test is: how does it feel? What does it do for your own internal practice? You can't turn over responsibility for your awakening to the science or the scientists' interpretation of it. Used in that kind of a practical sense, as a part of what is inevitably a first person practice, it's been incredibly useful. I was very skeptical, and I made my living being skeptical of science and I think rightly so. But there are limits both to the credibility that we want to give to science but also to the skepticism.

G: It's been so useful working with people, to say, "Look, here's what we know. Here are the top tier journals, good scientists, great institutions, and here's this study, here's this study, here's this study. They all fit together, and they all form a logical thread." That's compelling. It doesn't have to mean bowing down to it, but at least here's a consistent stream of highly-skilled people coming up with the same conclusion heading in the same direction. We've learned more at each step, it gets more informed, we get more sophisticated, more detailed... that it's been a consistent path. This is very useful, and people like that. When my brain first saw MRI scans of a meditating brain, it was—this is crazy—it was really fascinated by it. The brain was seeing for the first time that in fact this is what it had been trying to do. But now it could actually see what it has been trying to do.

R: The brain wants to see what it's doing.

G: Exactly, and it doesn't have any way to do that. But now it can stand back from itself and look at this thing.

R: It's helpful, it's illuminating. What is most illuminating is that there's nobody there doing the doing.

G: Exactly, it's obvious there isn't. We look for it. The "I" is an *ad hoc* entity. It's all over the place. There's no little homunculus sitting there in the middle directing things. It's just a bunch of energy patterns moving across the surface of the cortex.

R: But I can feel people going, "But-but-but you know, I-I

want to be the director of my own movie. Quiet on the set!" But if you just stay with it and realize what immense freedom that is, in a different sense, that you're free from there being that homunculus pulling those levers there... In fact you're this highly adaptive symbiotic relational being that's interacting with a highly complex cosmos, it's beautiful! It's not a loss that there's no center to it. In fact the idea that there's a center to it makes it kind of a drag.

G: It's like the Woody Allen movie. Remember? They were pulling the levers up above? That was the vision that we had of that. In fact, like you say, you find that people are so afraid of the whole thing of not having free will. We talked before about how it's the most freeing, liberating, empowering thing, surprisingly, that you could imagine, because you let go of this belief that you somehow can control things and must try to control things. Well it's impossible, you can't do it. You're not even there.

R: Right, you're nothing but the cosmos surfing with itself.

G: That's right.

R: Which is beautiful, though, because when you try to direct the surfing and you keep falling off, you go, "What's wrong with this! Why did God create a being that can't surf?"

G: You keep yelling at yourself internally, disciplining yourself...

R: Doing nothing but.

G: (laughs)

R: You idiot! Get back on the board!

G: That's right.

R: So not only can the "I" not dance, it can't surf.

G: It can't surf either.

R: How about: it just isn't.

G: It isn't. It isn't even there... scientifically.

The wonderful surprises of awakening beyond thought

R: Surprise!

G: Surprise!

R: Um... surprise.

G: Yes, I thought we'd maybe talk about surprises that we found in the course of our spiritual practices.

R: Such a long list, which is part of the surprise... I think.

G: (*laughs*) Yes.

R: Surprise number one is that it's not a thing, that it's not an experience to be had. Also, that this phenomenon of not being an experience to be had actually allows you to deal with endless ongoing surprises, right? It's not so much that they don't occur—I think it's a common expectation that negative things would just stop happening and that there would be celestial music that would accompany each moment (although there is). Instead surprises no longer appear as a surprise or as so shocking, and yet at the same time the joy and novelty of life only intensifies. This absence of any end point or final experience per se actually deepens and almost renders it more joyful in its ongoing activity.

G: It's one of the mistakes that a lot of people make, pedagogically as it were, that they think it's a gold medal event. It's an Olympic gold medal that they can claim and pin around their neck and wear a little badge of some sort. In fact, as you point out, that's one of the most limiting things you could do. The last thing you'd want to do in an unfolding process, an awakening process, is to freeze it by saying, "Okay, you've won the gold medal, now that's it", because then you're kind of locked into this place of "Okay I'm done now". You find out that things keep changing. So I must not have been done before, or else I'm doing something wrong because I'm supposed to be this thing, and I must not be that after all.

R: So let me carry out some exercises in order to protect that thing that I thought I was going to be for a while.

I think the other surprise may be at just how ordinary it is. One experiences the ordinary as itself full of all kinds of miraculous capacity that appears to have been there all along. In the most mundane encounter, like in the middle of the night I was driving back from an airport, and I stop to get some fuel and some food. I meet somebody who is making me a sandwich. Because I'm there and not thinking, "Ohhh, what time am I going to get home?!", and, "How'd I get myself into this situation?" There's a really magical quality to the most ordinary of interactions. So, even though there isn't a "special" experience per se, there is a flavor and a richness to ordinary experience that exceeds any experience I could have ever imagined having achieved as a part of this process.

G: Yes. The sweetness we've talked about before that attends this being "now, now, now". Folk have said, "Well there's just past-present-future, and they're all the same, just the passing of time." In fact that's not the case, in my experience, nor I think in yours either, that this "now, now, now" thing has a tremendously different content to it, a richness to it, than past or future which are just storylines.

As you say the most prosaic, the most mundane possible thing happens and it's just ongoing, beautiful, fantastic, unfolding. So much deeper than anything you could ever have brought into that space before, no matter what you took in or out, or what you did or what your practice was.

R: Yes, so I suppose a kind of a corollary to that after ordinary, is simple. One of the refrains that I feel when I'm able to most let go and be in this space, is the surprising and, well, astonishing simplicity of it. It's really not an epically complex phenomenon. It's a phenomenon that is right within you at all times, you just never learned how to tarry with it and actually look there, right?

I was working with some people in an academic context last week and it felt like I was just pointing out that they had never looked at a particular place which was the ground of their awareness... they are always looking at some content of their awareness. Some of them were slapping themselves on the forehead and saying, "I just never looked there!" It's as if you've had a post-it note on your forehead your entire life and you never realized it was there.

G: Right, no one told you. Yes, exactly.

R: And the post-it note said, "Ordinary experience is totally miraculous if only you'll actually pay attention to it."

G: It's so close, it's so intimate, so even more than intimate. So right there, all the time, that you can't believe you looked past it for so long.

R: Yes. It's like you're going around the supermarket looking for some sort of item to put in your cart and the cart itself is the thing that you're looking to put in the cart. It's astonishing in its clarity and its immediacy.

G: We've also talked about how desires change, the nature of desire changes, because you don't have the flywheel of self-referential narrative thought to amplify every desire into a wild craving or every tiny slight into a raging episode. You really get back to just the biological amount of this that is not mediated by thought, and you can see that it's very different than what you thought it was.

R: Right. The very thing that probably launches many of us into any kind of inquiry or spiritual quest whatsoever is itself a kind of craving or desire. I want to feel better; I want to not feel that way. It really is surprising that I imagined that I was just going to be able to deal with those kind of cravings better, like I want sex, I want drugs, I want endless amounts of food, I want money. What is surprising is that those things all persist but the "I want" disappears, or at least asymptotically approaches zero. That is so surprising because we have this more or less bodily habit structure where we get into situations and our expectations are already there cued... "Okay and this is the time in which you will want... and action!"

G: That's right.

R: And then the wanting isn't there! (*laughs*)

G: And the wanting just doesn't occur.

R: That is maybe the most surprising thing that can happen, because those wants are so convincing. Even when you're thinking, "I'm working on transcending that, you know," implicitly we think of that in a repressive sense. We think, "Well, I'm just going to be able to control myself when these things come around" as opposed to the wanting itself being gone. It is different in some way that's hard to put into language, for the desire and the appreciation to be gone. Things are if anything more beautiful and attractive and astonishing. I don't resent money. I don't resent beauty. I don't resent material objects. I don't seek to negate them, they're just there and they either come into my field of awareness or they don't come into my field of awareness and there's no craving.

G: The surprising thing too is that if you take the central pleasures, like sex for example, it's much more acute, it's much more intense because you aren't mentally mediating it.

When it does pass your field nothing gets in the way of the pure experience. In the past there was always a storyline. If you try to enjoy almost anything, there always are all kinds of media-enhanced visions of how this should be...

R: Even if the media is just your noggin.

G: Exactly, exactly, exactly... But it's impossible to parse it out, until you say, "Okay, what if we just drop that?" This whole mental process falls away and then you're just left with pure experience.

R: Right. I think the way I might put it is that, before, part of the association of the craving is that sex or some other extraordinary experience was "always about to be"; it was incipient and I was on the trigger...

G: Always hunting...

R: Whereas now, as you point out, sex IS; capital "I", capital "S". You're not anywhere else, and then that IS-ness extends to everything else in your ordinary experience. Your cereal in the morning, IS. A cup of tea IS. And that IS-ness is so extraordinary that there's no room for craving. How could you possibly want anything else? The habit structure remains where part of your body kind of goes around and says, "Okay, now we're about to get our little hit of 'fill-in-the-blank'." No need.

G: Yes. The brain, as we've discussed, turns out to like this space, to prefer it. So it neurally enhances that and even dopamine-reinforces the situation because it does feel as if you become so content in this space—so totally "now, now, now", that movement out of that, whether it's the movement of thought or movement of desire or movement of fear, it just isn't interesting. It just isn't something that could come in and intrude in that space because the space is so compelling by itself.

Ramana Maharshi says that after a while you'll have a hard time thinking. It's difficult to make thoughts occur because the brain says, "Ooh, that's not cool. We don't want to do that. This space is so much better and so much richer than that."

R: But again, to be clear, it's a hard time thinking self-referential narrative thoughts as opposed to the incredible flow and stream of completely elaborated ideas that float by that I wasn't noticing before because I was too busy thinking about what ideas I had to come up with.

G: There's so much bandwidth consumed by self-referential "blah-blah"—98% of most people's bandwidth. The good stuff, the inspirations, problem solutions and the insights could hardly find their way through that maze to get recognized. Now you've got all this open bandwidth, and you're much more still, so you're more likely to be able to see one of these inspirations when they arise.

R: I think that's why, before, it felt like surprise was a rare event. Some of those already elaborated ideas, which might be "aha moments" leaking through or sneaking through the self-referential thoughts like, "Don't bother me I'm coming up with an idea!"… If people will meditate or pause on it, think about what it feels like when you feel surprising thought come into being, that is the closest to the feeling-tone of how it feels almost all the time, right?…You know something is coming in out of nothing.

G: Right, right.

What is a teacher?

R: One of the questions that I struggled with for a very long time was this question about the role of a teacher...

G: Oh, yes.

R: ... in the cultivating of non-dual awareness. I pause and give gratitude for that experience, because on the one hand I knew upon reflection that I have been blessed with so many incredibly great teachers going back to my kindergarten experience. I pause and give gratitude for that experience. But there's a different valence in mystical practice of non-dual traditions where people will talk about the necessity of a certified teacher.

I also incorporated the news that I was constantly seeing about teachers and their abuse of that position that seems to be endemic and not really the fault of the individuals involved. I was wondering what your perspective was on that.

G: Well there are a couple of really good questions there. Teachers in general, um, there's some famous stories but... The main thing is that everybody's a teacher.

R: Yes.

G: Ramana Maharshi's been enormously important in my awakening and in my life; he's been tremendously useful for me. But, it can be the person in the supermarket line, somebody at the DMV, somebody you run into at Starbucks, one of your students in your classroom. Teachers don't have to come with dreadlocks and black robes and long beads and such. Teachers' messages come from all kinds of places. We talked about bibliomancy—a book pops out the shelf, one you just "have to read". Now that's a teacher. That book has been delivered to you and is there for some reason.

R: Uh-hmmm.

G: Who was the teacher there? Well, the book. Yes, but what moved the book into my presence in a way that I could work from it? I really don't compartmentalize people off into teacher boxes. I try very hard not to become "a teacher" and to have any "up and down relationship". For me it's much more... we're all "Her" dancing, we're all One thing. And so... "get over it people". Really, get over it, and just recognize that we're all here together—trying to work our way through this thing, to share as much as we can and to learn as much as we can from every place and everybody we can possibly learn from.

R: Right. I always knew that intuitively. There's a black walnut tree out the window that has been one of my great teachers.

G: Yeah, yes, exactly!

R: The whole cosmos is a teaching entity in my experience.

G: Absolutely.

R: One of the downsides of saying "Ah okay, I've found this teacher!" is that it blots out all of the other teaching, whatever the merits of that particular being. We don't see what's right in front of us.

G: Exactly.

R: The teaching is in fact about being with, and learning from, what is right in front of us.

G: Exactly.

R: At the same time I do love and practice what I call spiritual friendship, for lack of a better term, and I'm open to a better term for it.

G: Oh, sure.

R: Within the collective of people that are themselves experiencing the way in which consciousness is something much larger than themselves, one comes across people, again, often very serendipitously, like the opening of a book. You and I came into contact serendipitously.

G: We did.

R: There's just a feeling where you say, "Oh yes, there seems to be some sharing happening here." And that sharing that really seems to be there a great deal of the time, rather than an up-down modality.

G: Yes.

R: If I've ever had any kind of blockages in either learning from other people or having them learn with me, then there's been some kind of unconscious or implicit assertion of this up-down relationship.

G: Absolutely, absolutely. We talked earlier about money for teaching...

R: Yes, I'll pay you later.

G: That's one of the pernicious parts of exchanging money even if it's only 15 cents.

R: Right.

G: That does establish "up" and "down".

R: Mmmhmmm.

G: As you teach as a very effective professor, the fact that you're in the front of the classroom, you're getting paid to teach them and they're paying tuition to be there, it's difficult to work across that because you're put up there socio-culturally and from an academic standpoint. I know you're very good at it, getting alongside them, being one with them and understanding exactly where they're coming from, working with them in really unusual ways. But, many of your peers want to be "up here".

R: I have peers?

G: There are many people who want to be "up here" and they want you to be "down here"—that really does freeze the amount of communication that can take place.

R: Yes and it locks people into roles where one is the transmitter and one is the receiver or…

G: Knower and not-knower.

R: And then what happens is that you just remain receiver until you become transmitter and then you replicate the whole transmitter-receiver operation, which must work for somebody, but I don't know who that person is.

G: One of the amazing things is when you've begun working with people it's amazing how much you learn from them.

R: Oh, yes.

G: This person comes to you and says, "Oh, I don't know anything, this person knows everything." No, not at all as you find out if you just open up, let go of this "up/down" thing and just be present. It's astonishing. Everybody has something to teach you. Everybody. And just be aware of that, not because you have to honor it, but because you keep seeing it over and over and over again. When somebody comes into my space I'm excited about what we can learn from each other!

R: Oh, yes.

G: You learn both ways enormously. There's a flow of inform-ation energy back and forth, communication.

R: Right. To go back to that example of bibliomancy, which as you know, is one of my favorite words... a book opens or falls off the shelf or you open a page at random and there's a passage that speaks to you...

G: Mmmhmmm...

R: And as you rightly put it, okay now who's the teacher there? Is it the book? It's the entire cosmos unfolding for 13.7 billion years that delivered that teaching...

G: That book to you at this time exactly when you needed it.

R: Right. And so one grows precisely to the extent that one can experience the teaching that's available in every dimension of one's life. And to the extent that one locates "a teacher" in "a place", almost inevitably we're going to lose sight of that fact.

G: Absolutely... absolutely.

When, where, why you get stuck on the "path"

R: Gary, do you find that people seem to learn and unfold in clusters when you're working with them and doing this sort of dialogue? I find that when one person is really lighting up on something, getting something, that somebody else maybe across the planet is also unfolding. That sometimes also happens in terms of this phenomenon of "getting stuck." I thought we might talk a little bit about what we've seen in terms of people making enormous progress and then getting stuck and what some tactics are for noticing that they were never stuck.

G: Yes, I think it's quite common for people to get some initial openings, begin to understand something and begin to make real progress. Then suddenly, you talk to them and it just stopped. They've stopped sitting, stopped practicing, stopped inquiring, stopped doing anything, and they've decided that there's a specific reason for that. What the reason really is, is they're afraid of going any further. Some part of their consciousness/ego/I construct has seen that this is really a kind of dangerous thing for its own employment, and so it says, "Well let's look at this a bit, let's calm down here, slow down, take some time to look around and, you know, just compare." And then, "Oh my goodness look at all this—I have a bunch of intellectual problems, questions and conflicts."

You can watch when people start to branch intellectually. It's the ego coming in and trying to say, "Hey look, let's... let's call this thing off, let's call off the search. I've had enough of this already, thank you very much... and all these questions

I've got about this thing!" I see that often. Do you too?

R: Yes, I do too. You're quite right. So often a lot of times it takes place on this cognitive level where there're all these theoretical reasons why this couldn't possibly work. There're all these aspects of one's life that one actually treasures, like, "I enjoy my suffering. Suffering's very important. I wouldn't be able to interact with my spouse if I didn't enjoy my suffering."

G: Right.

R: "That's authentic, that's real! I wanna live a real life!"... for example. My response is usually to just be with that and say, well, okay I can see the virtues of that. But the pattern is so predictable and repetitious, that it must be part of the phenomenon of the narrative mind getting the message and saying, "Hey, sales are down on stories about the "I". We need to get this division operating again!" (laughs)

G: (laughs) Yes, yes.

R: People might be able to feel their way out of that, right? They might recognize that, if they've read this book and say, "Oh, you know, I seem to be trying to throw a cognitive net over this." It can't be figured out by the mind.

G: No, absolutely not. These are common themes right now in the neo-advaitin community, which to me is the "faux-advaitin" community. Things like: "I love my suffering, I want to keep my suffering, I need my suffering so I can feel human." People have told me "You're not human!" I reply "Well, I kind of think I'm human... I may not be like how you are, but I don't need my suffering. Matter of fact, I didn't really care for my suffering when I had it around. I didn't feel I needed to have more of it. And so I thought it should be a good thing if I could get rid of it."

And yet, people say that, and several other lines you said. This cognitive dissonance comes in when the ego throws up any possible thing it can. There are enough people bumping up against this work now so there are a lot of stories floating around like, "Here's a big problem, these people aren't human!" or "They can't relate to other folks!" or "They can't live in the world, they can't function in the world." Which is just not true.

R: Yes.

G: It's just not correct. You don't need your suffering.

R: It doesn't appear to be the case. Frankly, if somebody told me I wasn't human, I would take that as high praise.

G: (*laughs*)

R: Look at the record!

G: Log on.

R: Yes. If what it means to be human is to make the same mistakes over and over again for thousands of years and to manifest those mistakes into the ecosystem, material reality and other human beings, then it's time to evolve, people. That kind of direct approach in my experience rarely works.

What concerns me, or what I have to be with, is that when the mind tries to grasp what has already occurred when there's been some opening, it can be, in my experience, extremely volatile. It's a kind of wheel spinning where you're saying, "Well, it's this!" Very quickly the mind sees that it can't do it. Then it says, "Well, it's not because I need my suffering, it's because I need to experience what it's like to both have suffering and not have suffering at the same time. So I need to be a bodhisattva, right?" Endless possibilities come out of those 100 trillion synaptic neural connections. The further along we get, the more quickly the mind exhausts the possibility that that's actually going to work, because we've had this experience which is ineffable, which we're all having right now.

G: Right, right.

R: The reason I want to share this is just out of compassion. I feel it with the people that I work with, as sometimes they get all strung out trying to figure this stuff out. Just relax, float downstream, feel what it feels like to be in that silence and just be good with the fact that it's not a crossword puzzle that you can figure out.

G: Well, and the feeling, you mentioned feeling. That's one thing that people have to really understand. This is a very tactile, sensory journey. Your default position should be, "How do I feel when I'm not in blah, blah? When I'm not suffering? When I'm not in confusion and anxiety? How does it feel?"

If they can get that feeling and go back and forth enough times, the brain looks at that and says, "This is way cool and that other thing is not cool anymore." That can be your antidote for all of this intellectual, never-ending philosophizing, analyzing, categorizing. You can go on the web and get ten zillion different sources for this stuff. You're your own way out of this thing. This really is DIY.

You can feel your way through this thing; I did. Just feel what feels best for you. This is all about your being really happy in a different way than you were ever happy before. Just feel what it's like when you have that space, just go there and then see the contrast. Your mind will never be able to touch this space. The problem that the ego has is it can see that it can't get to that space and it's frustrated, it doesn't know what to do. So it begins to analyze the whole thing. Just trust that.

R: Yes, so it calls it emptiness or the void or...

G: Yes the void or the Dark Night of the Soul or blah, blah, blah, whatever. It's just the mind running around trying to save its job.

R: Right, it's like words running around trying to describe the taste of an orange or the smell of a rose or...

G: Yes!

R: It doesn't mean there's anything wrong with language or anything wrong with the mind... It's just that it's a mistake to expect that kind of capacity out of either of them.

I think that one of the most important things that you just said was being with feeling, that feeling really is the way you're going to find your way out of there. When you are experiencing that volatility and the mind is grasping for any narrative, explanation, theory or insight that is going to make sense of what is—that's when you can get behind it by just feeling whence comes that kind of scatterbrained attempt to make sense of it. When you get there it doesn't matter if it's scatterbrained, you just feel the silence out of which even that volatility is coming.

The other thing that can't be said often enough is that it's DIY. It has to come from inside. You have to become a lamp unto yourself. Yes, you can have spiritual friends—there's even a kind of a global sangha of sorts that's emerging. But the sangha emerges on the basis of us all knowing that each of us has to feel our way to the truth in this pathless land. We can't take what anybody else says is really a way to orient our journey except as a way of debugging something that we feel ourselves is a problem.

G: Yes. The big pushback I get on DIY is, "Well how do you know you aren't fooling yourself?" Nobel Laureate Richard Feynman's quote: "The first principle is that you must not fool yourself, and you're the easiest person to fool" is very useful. So they ask, "How do you counter that?"

It's a very simple thing, and it's what I used all the way along; I said, "Okay, am I done thinking yet?" "No." Okay... then you aren't done yet so you just keep looking back for self-referential thoughts. If you have these problematic thoughts, you're not done yet. The mega-check is, "Are you still suffering?" If you're still suffering and if you still have a lot of self-referential thoughts, there's more work you can do.

I had two Zen masters I could go to at the end for a "pass/ fail" evaluation, but they were of little value to me in the process because they had not done this approach. You know if you're suffering, better than anybody else in the world will ever know. If you're suffering, you can get rid of that, really.

R: What's beautiful is that Feynman, the physicist, probably gave too much credence to the idea that you can BS your-self because there's less respect in post-WWII physics for the internal world than there is for the external world. Whereas the example you just gave shows that it's actually not possi-ble to BS yourself if you will turn your awareness back and look from whence any thoughts are coming and observe your thoughts. That can't be faked. It's like, are there fish in the aquarium or not? (*laughs*)

G: (*laughs*)

R: You know, if you look back at the...

G: And there are fish there?

R: ... and there're fish in there ...

G: Get out your fishing rod.

R: ... get out your fishing rod and just dissolve them. Be with them and watch them disappear. The real strength, to me, is that you know full well whether or not you're BS-ing yourself.

G: That's right.

R: What's beautiful about that is that after a while it just becomes automatic and it's just like, "Oh, there was a fish... a little fish."

G: That's right.

R: Welcome.

G: The key is not to get caught up in the fish.

R: Right.

G: The thing is to recognize the fish are there. Fish aren't evil. But you need to say, "How can I get rid of these fish?" It just goes back to the subject. Who is seeing the fish? Forget about the fish. Go back to who is seeing the fish and begin asking, "When is she here? What does she think? Where does she live?" Just begin to understand what it is that's seeing the fish.

R: Whence comes the aquarium.

G: Whence comes the fish, whence comes the aquarium? You can keep running this check back.

R: Right and that's why Ramakrishna, who is from that Advaita Vedanta tradition, would always say, "Keep going."

G: Keep going. Yes.

R: There's no error in constantly looking back at one's thoughts. There's no problem with observing thoughts and there not being any there.

G: That's right.

R: There's no downside to it.

G: It's a very sweet place.

R: It's the sweetest.

G: One last quick point. Another trap is getting a badge. If you get a badge, say you get your green belt, yellow belt, or black belt...

R: Where's mine?

G: ... and you become trapped in being that title—you're enlightened or you have some fancy title.

R: Epaulets.

G: Epaulets... yes, or nice, big beautiful hats. That's the worst thing that could happen to you because you get stuck there and you know in your heart of hearts when you look back inside there are fish in the aquarium. You know there are fish in the aquarium! You may have fooled everybody else, but you know there're still fish in the aquarium. You are your own only possible check back.

R: Right, and you're so busy staring at the epaulets or the badge that you forget to look back, and then the fish...

G: The fish are all over the place!

R: Fish are schooling, pretty soon it's a feeding frenzy.

G: (*laughs*) Exactly!

R: And... (*laughs*)

G: Piranhas! (*laughs*)

Why the resistance to having fewer narrative thoughts?

R: Incredulity. It's actually a great experience to be incredulous. It gets you kind of knocked out of your state of belief, which is more or less what it indicates. But I've been really interested watching on the sidelines at people's responses to your narrative of "the end of thought". And so…

G: Ahhh. And they're incredulous.

R: Yeah they're incredulous! (*laughs*)

G: (*laughs*) They remain incredulous! Start incredulous, they remain incredulous.

R: It's really, really interesting. So I just sort of wanted to open up on it. First of all it seems like it's an opportunity that is quite beyond the merit or otherwise of the incredulity—it's an opportunity for everybody because of the power of that incredulous response. When you're truly incredulous you experience a "No freakin' *wayyy*!" that opens up that possibility for a kind of nanosecond of thought, where you turn around and say, "Hey, who's incredulous? Who wonders about the possibility to turn off a part of our brain?" That gives this opportunity, which is always there of course, to tap into Source. Just assuming that opportunity has not been taken, because again when I've watched people respond to your narrative—which I'm not even characterizing as a claim, you're giving a narrative about what happened when "you" dropped away… Then this second order thing that becomes interesting is why, of all things, are we incredulous about, this? You can find credulity about just about anything out there... you can believe six impossible things before breakfast.

G: (*laughs*)... anything! The most absurd things!

R: Well, the more absurd, the better in a certain way, and that might be a clue to why the incredulity comes in at this point, rather than with those other things. But I just wondered if you wanted to talk at all about the incredulity with which people greet the possibility that you really can turn off, for all intents and purposes, your narrative mind and experience what it's like.

G: A couple of things... your point about that the more incredible it is, the more likely it is to be accepted in normal parlance. Not so long ago we went through the "12-12"/ "12-31" thing, that the world was going to end and people were going to come from some planet back behind some star and land on the Earth. Many people believed that whole thing.

R: You ruined it Gary! They're not ready to come out now, because you keep doing this!

G: (*laughs*) Right, I keep doing this and putting them back. But many people believe that! We saw this exhibit at Penn where they showed that it's not what the Mayan calendar says. This loss of narrative mind would seem to be a logical extension of what we do every 24 hours: we go to sleep and we lose our narrative mind. We wake up the next morning and then we start to crank it up again so the narrative mind's there. Every night we look forward to falling asleep and having this period of having no narrative thought. We love it, prepare for it, buy special platforms, special pillows and everything else.

R: Devote about one-third of our lives to it.

G: A third of our lives to it, and we love it!

R: I don't have time for that!

G: (*laughs*) I don't have time for that! No, and so you think that would dawn on folks; look, this happens anyways. You know if they watch, most people when they're talking, their narrative mind doesn't go on. When they're with a friend they just keep talking. They're not thinking up each individual words they say—it just comes out. So there's a period when they don't have narrative thought. Ninety-nine percent of their waking life is consumed with this self-referential "I-me-my" storyline that's episodic, autobiographical, "She's gonna say this, she said that yesterday..." It never stops and causes all kind of bad problems... You'd think people would welcome a break from it.

But it varies with the audience. I've talked to groups where they said "That's really interesting!" I remember this one woman who was a reporter for CNN in Hong Kong, and she was really fascinated by it... "Is that possible? Really?" She was really curious about it. It ranges from that, to people who say, "It's just impossible. You must be lying, you're at best deluded." There is a big pushback.

That is the real ground of the ego, this I-me-my thing. You're coming onto its turf and saying, "We're gonna shut you down." Or, depending on how open they are, as you were saying, how self-reflective, they're turning back and asking, "Who's saying that?" As you look carefully, then you're right into the face of the ego. This is its game, what it does for a living. If you begin to challenge the possibility that it doesn't need to be there, it'd have a much smaller or no role at all, it's a big threat.

R: The analogy you draw with sleep is interesting because if I came in here and claimed, "Hey, I had no dreams!" you wouldn't say, "Oh, come on! Impossible!"

G: "You can't be serious!"

R: "Did you eat chili before you went to bed?"...

G: "You're lying!"

R: In all likelihood I probably forgot the dreams that I had, but the point is that it's not an enormous claim to say that I didn't have any dreams last night. In fact the opposite, to say like, "I had this dream"…

G: "Oh yes, tell me about it, tell me!" (*laughs*) "Let's analyze it, let's analyze it!"

R: (*laughs*)… exactly. It's yummy, you know, for the imagination. Yes, let's talk about our dreams. So to flip it around and see that it's possible to experience everyday life devoid of dreams, the dream of the "I"… It's odd that it would produce this response. That's why I'm going slowly on it… it's obvious who's responding to the claim.

G: Right, right.

R: This saying, "Um, I think you're in my territory here. Under no circumstances will you listen to this story because…"

G: That's right… inadmissible in this court.

R: Exactly, it's *a priori* ruled out!

G: It's ruled out. Right.

R: Right. But when we take one other step back and say, well maybe it's worth not being incredulous about this claim, that the one who is so incredulous about the possibility that we could have a dreamless sleep…

G: Right, yes, during the day.

R: … during the day is worth looking at, right? That could become a real opportunity to use the virulence of the response. To look at who it is that objects so strongly to the claim that you can turn off your narrative mind, you can surrender the narrative mind, and you can experience something far more enjoyable than the constant piloting by the narrative mind.

G: Ramana Maharshi talked about his being asleep while being awake. That's the metaphor he was trying to draw. You do this every night, why should it be a big deal to have it not happen during the day? It's like being asleep while awake. You're walking around and yet it's quiet. People say, "OMG, I just can't imagine not having that going on, and you know losing some of my swings of sensations, my highs and my lows... I just can't imagine living life without that, it must be horrible!"

And yet, as you've found, and many others have found, it's really sweet. It's a lot better than anything else you can come up with, which is why the brain stays there. If it wasn't—then the brain wouldn't stay there, it would keep running out to things. But it does find this sweeter place. You don't give up anything, you gain something.

R: The analogy that comes to mind is that we're all in some collective living situation. There's a TV there that's unavoidable and it's just constantly showing soap opera with the highs and the lows. Everybody is transfixed and somebody says, "Would you turn it off? There's this switch..."

G: "No, no, no, don't turn it off!"

R: "There's a switch there." Then, "There's no switch, that's impossible!"

G: "There's no switch there!"

R: "That *is* where we are! How could there be a switch to turn it off?" It's like, "Well, I've turned it off. You guys were all asleep, I came down here in the middle of the night..."

G: And turned it off.

R: "... I turned it off. It's amazing!"

G: "No!"

R: "Just check it out... there's this stuff that you can experience behind the show!"

G: "No!"

R: "It's called silence... it's really, really primo stuff." "Outrageous! How would we get anything done?" (Not that we are!) (laughs)

G: (laughs)

R: No. I think that's really it. If we can turn your story away from something that people should either believe or disbelieve—it shows that many of us are stuck in this position of either we want to buy it in both senses of the term, or not buy it. We either believe it or we disbelieve it.

G: Right.

R: So if we disbelieve it, there's a kind of virulence of, "no thank you, you know, I don't want this!"

G: Right.

R: Whereas, what's really being offered here and has been offered in the traditions that you're pointing to, is a set of techniques for experiment. It isn't something to be believed in or not believed in.

G: As you know, this was for me a completely empirical journey; this was not a philosophically-initiated journey. I could see my suffering, and it appeared that my suffering was caused by my "blah, blah" in my head, and so I thought this is just unacceptable. There has to be a better way. This can't be how we're meant to live our lives. So I just launched off into a bunch of experiments, trying to find lab notebooks that somebody would give to me and say, "Here, try this thing, try this thing." And I just kept trying things. The big turnaround was Ramana Maharshi's saying, "Look at the person! Look at the subject. Forget the objects."

R: Who's the experimenter?

G: Who's the guy running the experiments? You start doing that and it does start to deconstruct, and it is possible to just have those things fall away. Even if they don't go a hundred percent, if you can just break them down to where they're less virulent, if they're less addictive, perhaps get them down to thirty-five percent of the day you spend in stillness? That's so much better, in my humble opinion, than what most people take for their normal everyday life. I don't know why it isn't so compelling to folks. There's such a tremendous resistance to it.

R: For me a useful analogy is the idea of spiritual fitness. That, you know, "There's no possible way you can run an ultra-marathon!" where people are running for twenty-four hours. That's not really the issue is it? It's, "Can you ride your bicycle to work and back?" If you ride your bicycle to work and back, you start to notice that you're not spending all of your time in this kind of labored embodiment, which makes a huge difference. It's not the difference between being your former self and being Lance Armstrong, because that would require much more effort and technology. But it's such a massive difference that it might as well be infinity on the physical fitness level.

The way you experience the world once you have some level of fitness versus when you're really spiraling down in a negative feedback loop is so enormous that the word 'health' is not really adequate for it. Similarly, just making a little bit of headway in terms of what your spiritual or cognitive fitness is, in terms of spending all of your time and bandwidth in things like, "Oh, my boss is gonna do this!"... and then, "Oh, that bastard, I'd better do this!"... You have all this background stuff going on, "What if the Steelers don't win?" Then you

223

start to just let go of it, just a little bit… it's like everyday life as a kind of beautiful hot tub of bliss! (*laughs*)

G: (*laughs*)

R: Just by comparison, just by removing some level of the pain and the irritation. It's almost like the idea of the "I" or the egoic self, as chronic inflammation? You're living with this inflamed aspect of yourself and you believe it to be who you are. But if the inflammation just goes down a little, it's like the difference between having a full-on headache from a hangover and just a little pressure in your sinuses? I'm just offering these analogies because I myself am incredulous at the incredulity since, as I think one of your interviews pointed out, all of the mystical traditions point to this possibility. And now, neuroscience points to this possibility.

G: Yes, right.

R: If you were making some sort of huge claim and making people send in $19.95 before midnight tonight, then I'd say, "Yeah, you should be incredulous!" But there is no such thing. There's just the simple offer that, hey, newsflash—this is possible.

G: Well one thing that is happening, is, as I put in a blog post, one guy I've been working with for a year, just emailing back and forth… He has a full time job and had two years of not very engaged meditation. Just by beginning to question, which he did very diligently.

R: Self-inquiry.

G: Self-inquiry, he did very diligently, and lo and behold, he's got a lot of opening in the course of a day. He's lost a lot of stress, a lot of pressure, and he's functioning more efficiently. So, I think the misleading part about my journey was that it took 20,000 hours, maybe I'm just a slow learner, but I didn't have anybody to really talk to, to begin to work through...

R: There were no videos or books.

G: There were no videos (*laughs*), YouTube was decades in the future. But it's just the fact that you know that it's possible and that it doesn't take 20,000 hours... that you can do it in a lot less than that. This guy did practice part-time basically, and in the course of a year he unwound the thing. So this is not rocket science, it's very simple, it's very easy, and you can do it at work. I don't know why we're having the resistance.

R: But that's why there's incredulity, because speaking from my own experience, what I found completely shocking about my own openings, for lack of a better term, was how simple it was. I found it difficult to accept since my ego loves complexity. It just munches it.

G: Oh yeah, thrives on it.

R: Yes, and saying, well actually it's quite simple, was almost the most difficult thing that I had to work through... my love and fetish for, "It's gotta be like this and then it's gotta be like that...". It couldn't possibly be just, "Hey, turn around and look at who you are." There's a *bhakti* poet from the fourteenth century, in this wonderful *Oxford Anthology of Bhakti Literature*, who says, "No one understands me. It's too simple."

G: Yeah, exactly. It is just too simple.

Working with relationships, emotions and grief

R: How do relationships change as you get more into the awakening process?

G: We meet with storylines, as you know. I meet you or I meet somebody, and I have a storyline about the last time when I met this person. So what happens then is that their storyline meets my storyline. Their bag of perceptions around the neural network which codes "me" into their consciousness meets mine. So we never really come into contact with each other. We're just going neural network to neural network.

R: Your story gets together with my story and we'll work it out!

G: That's right, work it out, yes. Call my story and we'll schedule something.

R: (*laughs*) Yes.

G: Yes, exactly.

R: I've actually experienced this perceptually in the past that, if I was having an issue with what I thought was a relationship, I would close my eyes and I would feel an extraordinary distance from that person, like they were so far away. This gets represented in pop songs, but I think it's based on a perceptual phenomenon that is actually correct, that we can be in physical proximity but because we're actually mediated through symbolic frameworks that are accrued and not subject to our creative awareness, in fact all that's really happening is our symbolic carapace is getting in contact with the other's symbolic carapace. Sometimes the symbolic carapaces love each other and they say, "Oooh, your story matches my story!"

G: For a while.

R: Yes, Scorpio, Libra, right?

G: (*laughs*) Yes I get it.

R: But inevitably it's then just the stories—no story can really be made of that, right? Aristotle noted that any good drama requires a conflict. It's as if those stories are self-propagating machines, almost living things. They need conflict then in order to keep going as a story. Whereas if, through daily ongoing practices, you are able to begin to just be with reality, then astonishingly enough a lot, if not all, of the conflict disappears. Difference maybe emerges where somebody sees/experiences something one way another experiences something the other way but it's not a problem if it doesn't fit into the symbolic framework. So I would feel like the human gift of language and of narrative is both our greatest gift and our greatest curse because we begin to actually live in it instead of experiencing what reality has to manifest for us.

G: Well as you touched on that, if you can be very still when the story of this person that you meet comes up, you can watch the story come up, you can watch expectations arise, and if you're fully present for that, then the story kind of starts to wither away. The neural networks say, "Well, is this important? Is this image you have really useful?" And if you just don't take delivery on the package, then Hebbianly, the connections start to wither away.

R: Darwin puts it in the trash.

G: Exactly! Edelman, in his theory of Neural Darwinism, suggests that our neural networks select out which ones are going to survive or fail, based upon how useful they were. So from that standpoint, if you are very alert for emotions that arise, memories that arise, relationship stories that arise, and just don't take delivery on the package—don't buy into the storyline and let go of it, in fact that network will start to break down. As it does, then you can see your relationship improve as you have less and less of that carapace that you talk about.

R: Yes. This can be true in personal relationships and also even in the most superficial work relationships, which seem superficial because on some level they are, but they also actually have an enormous footprint in your life. As you were speaking, a kind of image came to my mind that as you encounter someone from your work world or another aspect of your world that feeds into any positive or negative pattern, any pattern whatsoever, you imagine it's like you're receiving a special package, like you said. You have to sign off on it. You can say, "OK, who's sending this feeling, and to whom is it directed? Okay, well… return to non-existent sender!" (*laughs*)

G: (*laughs*) There's no one here to get that package!

R: I'm sorry, nobody here by that…

G: Nobody, nobody here by that name.

R: It's just in that pause that the work takes place instead of the automatic "Let's pick up where we last weren't!"

G: Yes, exactly… yes.

R: Over time you start to see that these beefs, these accrued grudges and ideas of past advantages or disadvantage, begin to just disappear. It's not as if the people disappear, but you encounter them just as people.

G: As we've done with *Nirvana Shatakam* by working with

it, you can look at all these things. You can pull them out and you can probe… "OK, well how do I feel about Marcy?" When Marcy "codes in", you can feel what comes along with that coding in. Then you can just be present for that, be very empty for it, and lo and behold, the thing starts to unravel like a peeling onion, begins to get weaker and weaker and weaker. You can take anything… big pains in your life, big stresses or events you had, and they'll all unravel in the same way.

R: Strangely enough it can seem fine… I can do that with superficial instances in my life, but not the big ones! Like when I think of grieving a lost loved one, for example. But in fact, in some kind of strange way, it's easier and more effective on the big ones because you get an immediate kind of positive feedback loop to it. If you, instead of saying, "Ohhh, how I miss him!" say to yourself, "There are feelings of grief present, let me be with that grief. What is grief? What does grief feel like?", there's a kind of beauty that the grief takes on, or the regret takes on.

G: Yes.

R: You see the grief or regret as just grief or regret, as part of life. They have a beautiful aspect to them, as opposed to, "Ohhh, I can't feel that, I can't deal with that!"

G: Right. As you were saying earlier, it appears that we get dopaminergically-reinforced letting go. If you got a big peak of emotion from some big story and as you say go into it, and you can begin to work with it, you just don't take delivery on the package, you actually feel good. You can feel the letting go taking place, and it could only be neurotransmitters. Something is released to reinforce that letting go. Maybe the brain wants the real estate, whatever, but it feels good to go into those fears, go into those deep stresses and old pains and invite them in, have them in for a cup of tea and be present with them and just see what happens. You may find it's not an awful thing—it may be a very sweet thing to let go of that story.

R: There's a Rumi story on this one, the Sufi Persian poet, where he talks about the importance of just welcoming all emotions and feelings as guests.

G: Yes.

R: You say, "Ah yes, come on in."

G: Come on in, come on down.

R: Rather than feeling a need to repress... that there are parts of life that need to go away and that life would be good if only they didn't exist, instead you can see the beauty of regret. That it has its own feeling-tone, a feeling that has its own beauty and that is part of a complete life.

G: It's very important to focus on each particular instance, because each instance has its own character, tone and feeling and mixture of fear, anger, hostility and love and it's all bonded together. So you go into those, maybe coded through a person or a relationship, and you can feel, as Marcy lets go, what's in that texture. You don't have to analyze it—just recognize it. Don't take delivery on it and it's surprising how freeing it is to open into that. People say, "Well I can't possibly face that fear as it is just too horrible. I can't think about losing Fred or something." But yet, you go into that and there's great beauty to that, and you keep letting go, letting go—it really is a beautiful process.

R: I think it was very important that, as you just pointed out, each instance of it is totally unique.

G: Right.

R: I think part of the fear with grief is that one is going to forget Fred, for example. But actually by being with the feeling of loss, remorse or regret associated with that person, you're actually doing the opposite from forgetting that person.

G: That's right, you're honoring that.

R: You're totally honoring Fred in his Fred-ness, and being with it, but in a way that allows you to integrate it, rather than in a way that keeps you in this endless cycle of forgetting and remembering.

G: Right.

R: Then what's beautiful about each one of these instances of just getting behind an emotion that one thought one had to keep away, is that that actually allows the uniqueness to come through. When we feel uniqueness that is the feeling of oneness. We see that there really is/was/could never be any other who was like Fred. When we feel that oneness that is the feeling of the Oneness of the cosmos itself.

G: Absolutely. Yes.

Endnotes

1. Chanting for non-dual awakening

Chanting has a surprising power to move one "forward" in the process of non-dual awakening.

Chanting for non-dual awakening is focused on this simple guideline: watch where the chant arises and where it disappears. That is where the "action" is, where the "truth" is to be found. A simple shift of focus, but a profound one. The same approach is suggested for meditative inquiry: see where the I-thought comes from, and where it disappears into.

An example, from Happiness Beyond Thought: a Practical Guide to Awakening, is a Vedic classic, 'Asato Ma':

Asato Ma

Asato	ma	sat	gamaya
Non-being	to	being	lead me

Tamaso	ma	jyotir	gamaya
darkness	to	light	lead me

Mrtyur	ma	amritam	gamaya
Ignorance	to	eternal bliss	lead me

This chant is an asking to be led from the non-being of ignorance to the beingness of realization, from the darkness of worry, ignorance and confusion to the light of understanding, and from the "death" of not-knowing to the eternal bliss of knowledge.

Classically, this request was made to your guru, God, or higher power. In this work it is your personal "ego/I" asking for help to awaken. It's your "self" beseeching your Self for guidance. This can be a powerful surrender, a recognition that you can't do it all by yourself.

Chanting is more effective if your breathing is focused. Inhales are done from the "bottom up", i.e. first using the diaphragm/belly, then the ribs, then the upper chest. Exhales are done "top down", i.e. first using the upper chest, then the ribs, and then the diaphragm/belly. This gives a longer, more even chant; it is how opera singers get those long smooth notes.

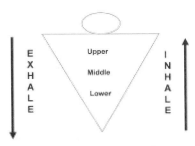

Breathing Pattern for Chanting

The meditative impact is strengthened if each line is chanted on one out-breath, followed by a silent inhale. An alternative approach is to chant a line on the exhale and then whisper the next line on the inhale. A powerful approach, which is a workshop favorite, is to move sequentially inward with more subtle chanting on subsequent rounds, first chanting out loud, and then whispering, and then finally chanting internally in silence. These chants are done as many times as you are moved to do.

This end note is taken from Gary's blog www:happinessbeyondthought. blogspot.co.uk/2013/01/using-simple-chants-meditatively-for.html which gives a great deal more information and useful links.

There's in-depth information about chanting *Nirvana Shatakam—the six Verses on the State of Enlightenment, Freedom and Happiness* by Shankara—which we have mentioned in the main text, at this link: www.happiness-beyond-thought.com/legacy/backgroundtexts/ nirvanashatakam.html

You can also request pdf copies for both chants from: www.non-dualitypress.org

2. **Let an Oracular Bugle Herald** *Dialogues on Awakening Beyond Thought* by Swami Blahblahananda

As recorded in my unauthorized hagiography *Uncanny and Wondrous Signs of Profound Mystery Associated With My Birth and Its Aftermath*, written on the occasion of the sixth decade of this my likely final incarnation, my birth and its aftermath was, as with all of the sages, buddhas, *arhats* and bodhisatvas of my lineage, attended by uncanny and wondrous signs of profound mystery. Rainbow feathered celestial birds flocked to the site of my glorious first breath, roosting upon wish fulfilling trees wrought entirely of crystal geodes and butterfly wings, chanting Shankara's *Nirvana Shatikam* while casting their spectra upon the skies. Glow worms read aloud from treatises penned in unfathomable and yet intoxicating tongues lit only by the light of their own reflection, debating the finer points of the meaning of my birth in scriptural exegesis while smoking enchanted herbs from hookahs of purest and highly polished sandalwood in the high plateau of coastal Alabama. In feline celebration, tiger cubs did cannonballs from highest peaks into the deep alpine pools of moonlit aquamarine glacier melt, dining on Velveeta dipped corn dogs as bejeweled groundhogs looked on in profound contemplation.

Yet all of this, and much more recorded in *Uncanny and Wondrous Signs of Profound Mystery Associated With My Birth and Its Aftermath, With Special Reference to Velveeta (Volume 2)*, pales beside the sublime music that resounded as if to herald my manifestation between this samsaric envelope of earth and sky. Within the desolate expanse of crag, peak and glacier, carved by the incessant ravages of weather and time, there echoed a sound of such profound and enigmatic importance that even now it resounds in my Brobdingnagian ears as a cosmic and unceasing mantra.

Liberated since birth, I have been free to engage unfettered in an unceasing exploration of this glorious and yet untamed sound that sounds like nothing else, not even itself. It is freedom itself, liberation waves echoing the primordial logos from whence all of the Advaita saints, as well as corn bugles, telemarketing and cold beer, spring. My intensive inquiry has led me to certain fundamental insights regarding this sound which resists language and cannot be thought, and yet Is.

- Its harbinger is laughter. When laughter is near, the Sound of Sounds bugles between.

- To be heard, it must not be fathomed. To be fathomed, it must not be heard.

- Its favored habitat is dialogue. In the pure exchange of extemporaneous inquiry among equals, the sound of sounds, by necessity, abounds. Dialogue means "speaking though", and the sound very much speaks through dialogue.

It is, as Gary Weber and Richard Doyle discover in these exquisite *Dialogues On Awakening Beyond Thought*, a "sweet" sound, although of course it is not the opposite of "sour" or "salty" or "cheesy". To hear the sound, as these dialogues point out, it will not do to do nothing. This is not the enlightenment of an all-inclusive resort chaise lounge yoga retreat featuring tropical drinks with umbrellas, although of course, it is not the opposite of that either.

It is not as if the sound can be avoided, for the cosmos is nothing but a manifestation of It. You have no choice, so you might as well surrender to the sound, and even that surrender isn't any more a "choice" than it is a "corn bugle." As these dialogues, which I hereby recognize as part of the illustrious and auspicious Blahblahananda lineage, point out, you are in fact a rather glorious way for this sound to hear itself, and it is the blissful sound of the end of blah blah blah. Perhaps you are about to hear it.

Thus Uttered Swami Blahblahananda

Index

A

Abyss 24, 25
Adams, Robert 123
Advaita 66, 215
Alcohol 114, 170
Altruism/philanthropy/reciprocal 147, 148
Attachment/clinging/grasping 29-37, 48-51, 73, 109, 125, 130,
    175, 176, 179
Authenticity 15, 36
Awakening 11, 16-19, 23, 44, 110, 115, 125, 133, 141, 146, 150,
    163, 174, 188, 190, 194, 198, 199, 204, 226, 232-235
Awareness vi, 8, 21, 24, 27, 32, 60, 71, 88, 165, 200, 201, 204,
    214, 226

B

Beyond thought/No thought 78, 83, 101, 102, 133, 141, 152, 163,
    186, 198
Bhagavad Gita 111, 133
Big Bang 1, 6, 77
Bliss/joy 22, 63, 64, 71, 113, 115, 116, 198, 224, 232
Buddhism/Buddha 23, 24, 34, 66, 67, 101, 139, 154
Byron Katie/Sedona Method 117, 118

C

Chanting/chants 29, 30, 107, 136, 232-234
Chaos/chaotic 2-5
Christianity/Jesus/Bible 148, 184
Compassion 83, 96, 147, 156, 212
Complexity 2, 125-127, 225
Consciousness; primary and secondary 21, 24, 25, 39, 48, 49, 51, 61-66,
    71, 78, 88-90, 102, 103, 115, 116, 119, 129, 170, 171, 181, 206,
    209, 226
Cosmos 6, 8, 23, 85, 130, 157, 181, 196, 205, 208, 231

D

E

F

G

R

S

T

Books *from* Non-Duality Press

If you enjoyed this book you might be interested in other titles published by Non-Duality Press.

Dancing with the Void, Betty Camhi & Gurubaksh Rai
Dismantling the Fantasy, Darryl Bailey
Walking Awake, Steve Ford
The Timebound Traveler, David Newman
The Best Thing That Never Happened, Joey Lott
Falling in Love With Where You Are, Jeff Foster
Nothing to Grasp, Joan Tollifson
Falling in Love With Where You Are, Jeff Foster
The Wonder of Being, Jeff Foster
Only That: the Life and Teaching of Sailor Bob Adamson
Emptiness and Joyful Freedom, Greg Goode & Tomas Sander
Presence Volumes I & II, Rupert Spira
Oneness, John Greven
Awakening to the Dream, Leo Hartong
Goner, Louis Brawley
Already Awake, Nathan Gill
Being: the bottom line, Nathan Gill
Perfect Brilliant Stillness, David Carse
I Hope You Die Soon, Richard Sylvester
Be Who You Are, Jean Klein
Who Am I?, Jean Klein
I Am, Jean Klein
The Book of Listening, Jean Klein